Advance Praise for *Broken Trust*

This timely book gives a much needed perspective from both the victims and perpetrators, who are — in these stories — themselves victims.
> **— Patrick J. Carnes, Ph.D.,** bestselling author of *Out of the Shadows: Understanding Sexual Addiction* and noted speaker

As you can well imagine, *Broken Trust* is a very difficult book to read. The important trust that is broken is in the pledge of gospel ministers to follow fully the gospel values proclaimed and modeled by Jesus. Barring a miracle of grace it seems that some of these situations of fractured trust will never be mended. But the point is that we are all called to pray and work for just such gospel miracles. Mark, Patrick, and Sue have given us the opportunity to examine wounded brothers and their victims in various stages of coping and recovery. For continuing progress there needs to be dedicated involvement in the Church and wider community to foster genuine healing. There are not many more stark situations in which we are called to contemplate the victory Jesus willed to make available to all peoples over sin and death through His Paschal Mystery. **— Most Rev. John R. Gaydos,** Bishop of the Diocese of Jefferson City, MO

The truth that sets us free is not just theoretical and philosophical, but often feels much more like *simple honesty.* We must speak with honesty without seeking vengeance or creating more victims. Here is a book of such healing honesty. **— Rev. Richard Rohr, OFM**

This insightful book reintroduces the theme of forgiveness and reconciliation as a way forward for the Church in responding to the sexual abuse crisis. The stories stir in us the ancient memories of the Church about redemption, not only for individuals, but for the Church as a community of faith. By tapping into these deep sources of our tradition, we find the possibility of a hope which is totally undeserved because it is total grace.

— Most Rev. Blase J. Cupich,
Bishop of the Diocese of Rapid City, SD

Within the area of sexual abuse, this might be the most helpful single book you can read. I have not found anything that is as systematic, as sympathetic, as fair, and as insightful on this question. It lays out the anatomy of the disease, the devastation it does to its victims, and the complex array of factors that help trigger sexual abuse — all from the inside, with fairness and sympathy. Everyone should read *Broken Trust!* **— Rev. Ronald Rolheiser, OMI**

This work courageously and honestly reveals the human side of clergy sexual offenders while mirroring the tragic experience of their victims. When survivors see only the evil side of their abuser, an opportunity is lost. These accounts give real meaning to the term "cycle of abuse" and open new avenues to forgiveness and recovery. *Broken Trust* is a must read for those struggling to understand why priests abuse, why victims suffer, and why all sides are in need of healing.

— Susan Archibald, President, The Healing Alliance

These experienced authors have put a compassionate face on the abusers who have been mostly victims of sexual abuse themselves. They have described the depth and dynamics of therapeutic healing instead of a punitive approach. As restorative justice practitioners, we are concerned with the healing and accountability for the victim, offender, and the community. Hopefully, *Broken Trust* will create greater understanding of this complicated problem.

— **Linda Harvey,** Founder, Program Director,
Restorative Justice Council on Sexual Misconduct
in Faith Communities

This masterful look at woundedness, healing, and hope is a tour de force: a wonderful and searching study with far-reaching implications for so many. It's odd to call such a book a "page turner," but it is. No one reading these case histories can fail to learn or be changed.

— **Paula D'Arcy,** author and speaker

Broken Trust is a stunning book — compelling, moving, and inspiring. I appreciated its integrity — telling the heart-wrenching stories of those who had been abused and the terrible tales of the abusers, who look back in horror at what they had done. This book both challenges us to forgive and, most amazingly, shows us the way to make forgiveness possible. Everyone who cares about the future of our church should read this book.

— **Kathleen Kennedy Townsend,**
author of *Failing America's Faithful*
and former Lieutenant Governor of Maryland

BROKEN TRUST

BROKEN TRUST

Stories of Pain, Hope, and Healing from
Clerical Abuse Survivors and Abusers

Patrick Fleming
Sue Lauber-Fleming
Mark T. Matousek

A Crossroad Book
The Crossroad Publishing Company
New York

The Crossroad Publishing Company
16 Penn Plaza – 481 Eighth Avenue, Suite 1550
New York, NY 10001

Printed in the United States of America on acid-free paper

The text of this book is set in 11/16 Cheltenham and 11/16 Benguiat Gothic. The display face is Torino.

Library of Congress Cataloging-in-Publication Data
Fleming, Patrick.
    Broken trust : stories of pain, hope, and healing from clerical abuse survivors and abusers / Patrick Fleming, Sue Lauber-Fleming, Mark T. Matousek.
       p. cm.
    Includes bibliographical references.
    ISBN-13: 978-0-8245-2410-4 (alk. paper)
    ISBN-10: 0-8245-2410-1 (alk. paper)
    1. Child sexual abuse by clergy. 2. Catholic Church – Clergy – Sexual behavior. 3. Suffering – Religious aspects – Christianity. 4. Sexual abuse victims. I. Lauber-Fleming, Sue. II. Matousek, Mark T. III. Title.
BX1912.9.F54 2006
261.8′3272088282 – dc22

                                              2006029162

1 2 3 4 5 6 7 8 9 10   12 11 10 09 08 07

We dedicate this book to everyone
who is caught in the cycle of abuse.
May the cycle be broken, with healing for all.

He has sent me to bring
glad tidings to the lowly,
to heal the brokenhearted.
To proclaim liberty to the captives
and release to the prisoners.
To announce a year of favor from the Lord
and a day of vindication by our God,
to comfort all who mourn.

—Isaiah 61:1–2. Jesus quotes this
passage in the Gospel of Luke (4:18–19)
to summarize his work on earth.

One of the fundamental tasks of spirituality . . . is to help us to understand and channel our sexuality correctly. This, however, is no easy task. Sexuality is such a powerful (divine) fire that it is not always easy to channel it in life-giving ways. Its very force . . . makes it a force not just for formidable love, life and blessing but also for the worst hate, death and destruction imaginable. . . . It is the most powerful of fires, the best of all fires, the most dangerous of all fires, and the fire which, ultimately, lies at the base of everything, including the spiritual life.

—Ronald Rolheiser[1]

CONTENTS

mm mm mm

RESPONSIBLE RECOVERY

A Note from the Publisher

Broken Trust is perhaps the most difficult book you will read on the topic of the clergy sexual abuse scandals in the Roman Catholic Church. And for this reason, it is the most important book you will read to understand why priest abusers have abused those in their care, how survivors have survived the crippling horrors perpetrated on them, and why there is still reason to hope for the future of the Church and the people of God.

At The Crossroad Publishing Company, we believe that books can play a constructive role in the wake of the scandals. Finding the right book, however, has not been easy. Most manuscripts we have received on the topic have fallen into two categories: those that blame the Church for holding fast to things like celibate clergy or the structure of centralized authority, and those that blame "liberals" for corroding the Church from the inside out and the American bishops who "let" them.

When our staff first read the manuscript of *Broken Trust,* which was brought to us by the book's editors and ably shepherded and edited by Roy Carlisle, it's power was clear. In these pages we meet abusers and abuse victims, and we hear their stories as they wish to tell them — unfiltered by anyone else and unadulterated by any agenda other than the desire to speak the truth. Their stories are complex, painful, devastating. They are also healing and redemptive — noisier and quieter than we might expect, refusing to conform to what we think they ought to say. And that is as it should be — the stories are not ours to tell but ours to hear and learn from.

One crucial caveat is in order: To hear an abuser's story is not to condone the abuser's actions or even to trust the words and manner the abuser chooses to communicate the details. Even if imperfect — yes, even if at times distorted or self-serving — the stories of the abusive priests included in this book are facts in their own right. Is it not better for us to know, however imperfectly, the mind of the abuser, whether one thinks of him first of all as enemy of the church, fellow sinner, evil one, or beloved of God? If we insist on moving beyond euphemisms, can we afford not to bring to light the stories of these men?

Our hope — our hope against hope — is that, as greater light is shed on what previously occurred in the dark, that which scandalizes need no longer be a scandal. These stories can evoke not just our horror at the actions of some priests and members of the hierarchy, but resolve to be agents for change. Can we, in the midst of scandal, no longer encounter a stumbling block? If love is stronger than death, can faith — in Christ, indeed in the future of the Church — be stronger than despair?

FOREWORD

~~~~~~~~~~

The unmasking of reality is stunning. Exposure of grave sin is equally shattering.

Broken Trust is such a work.

God alone knows the damage suffered by youthful victims of sexual abuse by priests who committed grave sins by violating them.

Broken Trust is a difficult book to read because of its stark presentation of personal accounts of victims violated by priests in whom they had implicit trust. *Broken Trust* is difficult to read because of the frightful personal accounts of priest perpetrators guilty of sexual abuse of minors. *Broken Trust* is straightforward. It neither glosses over the immeasurable suffering and irreparable damage done to victims nor minimizes the sickness of priest perpetrators. *Broken Trust* is a harsh but humbling reminder to all bishops, of which I am but one, to be vigilant, compassionate shepherds.

Thanks to Mark Matousek (and his ministry partner, Father Bert Miller). Their unique ministry offers *hope* to priest perpetrators.

Regrettably, and irreparably, some priests have *Broken Trust.*

Most Reverend Gerald A. Gettelfinger
Bishop of Evansville, Indiana

16

One

WHY THESE STORIES
MUST BE TOLD

The storm that is the clergy sexual abuse scandal broke onto the American Catholic Church and the U.S. public in 2002. At various vantage points from within the storm, the three of us have seen it growing and coming upon us for almost thirty years, although it has been developing far longer than that.

All three of us, then, have seen the good, the bad, the ugly, the beautiful, and the tragic in how all parties involved have handled the priest sexual abuse scandal in the American Catholic Church. We believe that it is necessary and healthy that this storm has broken upon the Church. Victims are being heard, their stories told. They have found their voice. This is necessary for their healing. It also makes it more likely that everything will be done to protect the vulnerable, especially our children. The American Catholic Church and its leadership — bishops and leaders of religious orders — are finally coming out of their denial and changing their very dysfunctional — in some cases criminal — ways of handling the clerical sexual abuse problem. American society in general is also breaking out of its denial about the seriousness and pervasiveness of sexual abuse of minors by trusted adults of every kind. A saying we saw years ago on a poster is quite apt for the Church's current situation: "The truth will set you free…first, though, it will make you miserable." This is a miserable but requisite time and process for the Catholic Church in America and throughout the world. Though storms are chaotic, messy, and sometimes destructive, they are also cleansing and renewing.

◆ ◆ ◆

When we work with victims of abuse we often encourage them and even join them in their anger at their abusers; anger is a very important stage in their healing. We have wept with them, we have raged with them. Then in recent years, we found ourselves counseling the clergy abusers themselves. We remain angry at the abusive behavior these men have perpetrated on innocent people — especially children, adolescents, and vulnerable adults. What they have done is abhorrent, and we never allow any excuse or rationalization for their offensive, abusive behavior. Yet as we worked more and more with these perpetrators, we began to see the woundedness underlying their compulsive, abusive behavior. We came to realize that they too had a trauma and abuse history, which was the root cause of their behavior. (Research variously estimates that between 62 to 81 percent of sexual offenders were sexually abused as children or adolescents.[2]) We increasingly saw their emotional and spiritual pain, both from what they had done to their victims and from their original psychic wounds. In short, despite our anger at what they had done, we came to the sacred experience of meeting their inner selves and seeing their humanity, which we experience with all of our clients, abused and abuser alike.

In the media we hear a great deal about the abuse these priest perpetrators have committed, a few details about their lives, much information about the legal situation, and some commentary about what the bishops are doing or have failed to do in handling these priests and their victims. Each priest appears as a sad news photo of a man in black and in trouble. Not much is told about who these men are; about what may have caused them to go from dedicated priest to abuser; about how they may have been victims of abuse themselves. We never hear of the rest of their lives and ministries and whether there were times and places in their lives when they were caring, pastoral priests and men of God. We do not hear if these priests are ever sorry for what they have done, get help, stop their abusive behavior, heal, and achieve recovery from their compulsion.

It is too easy then to think of these men as monsters preying on our children, as particularly horrible monsters because they are priests who should, it seems, be not only as good as we are, but much better. The contrast between the holiness expected of priests and the awfulness of their abusive behavior makes their media portrayal more lurid. They have betrayed not only their parishioners' trust but also their expectations of them. In our professional work, however, we have come to know the real, flawed, sick, wounded and wounding, yet human men behind the headlines. In the therapeutic process of helping them end their compulsive, abusive behavior, we see these very human persons in totality. What we see would surprise most people.

A CYCLE OF ABUSE

From very early in our practice, one of our main concentrations was working with survivors of emotional, physical, and sexual abuse. A significant percentage of these clients were individuals who had been sexually abused by clergy: Roman Catholic priests, Episcopal priests, Protestant ministers of all denominations, rabbis, a few cases of sexual abuse by Catholic nuns. We also worked with many clients who were sexually abused by fathers, mothers, uncles, aunts, brothers, sisters, teachers, youth leaders, and neighbors. We know first hand, then, the pain of victims of sexual abuse — and the intensified and added pain of sexual abuse perpetrated by a member of the clergy. We have witnessed, treated, and experienced their depression, extreme anxiety, profound toxic shame, intrusive memories and images from the abuse, dissociation, and suicidal feelings, to describe only part of their pain. With victims of clerical abuse, we have seen their even deeper shame and guilt, their spiritual confusion and even alienation from God, and the deeper betrayal and wounded ability to trust. We have journeyed with numerous victims along the long road to healing and freedom. We have also worked with a few victims who could not fully heal and whose lives have been permanently scarred.

WHY TELL THE STORIES

Through our experience with these men and women, we came to believe that all of their stories, those of both perpetrators and victims, need to be told and their voices heard. Because of shame and fear, because of legal and financial ramifications, and because of criminal, civil, and canonical (Church) law, the perpetrators' voices have not been heard; their story is missing. These perpetrators have become non-persons, ironically, sadly, in the same position now as their former victims.

The stories of priest abusers need to be told for several reasons. The first is prevention. The more we know and understand these men, the more we will know how to protect children and others who are vulnerable. Church leaders who form and supervise future priests will know better how to screen and prevent the development of sexually abusive priests and brothers in the future. People often ask how this could have happened. How could such highly educated, highly motivated men, entrusted with the sacred role of spiritual leaders, end up as child abusers? Hopefully, these stories will shed some light on this tragic development.

The second reason for telling these stories is to promote a healing, if indirect, dialogue between abusers and victims. The charged, very adversarial media and legal climate that has developed around the priest abuse scandal, as well as the constraints of confidentiality, have prevented any healing communication between abuser and abused. In the limited number of situations where the abuser has been able to personally apologize for his abuse to the victim, we have seen healing for both parties greatly facilitated. Unfortunately, this does not often happen. We hope that victims in reading these stories will be touched and will learn that some abusers truly regret what they have done and the damage they have caused. Our prayer is that this will facilitate healing for the victims and provide them some measure of understanding and peace about what was done to them.

Telling the story, and having it heard with compassion, is historically the core process of, and prerequisite for, healing. The patient wants a physician to listen to the story of his or her health complaint. In psychotherapy, a significant part of the healing comes from the client relating to the therapist the story of the psychological problem and the story of his or her life, feeling listened to and understood. Part of the success of Twelve-Step programs such as AA is that the addict is invited to tell the story of the addiction, sometimes over and over. Telling the story, and listening to the story, brings clarity, insight, understanding, compassion for self and the other person, fellowship in a shared humanity, and a new vision of possibilities for change and renewal. In our experience, when a victim of abuse hears something of the story of the abuser, it can be powerfully healing for the victim. Victims may no longer feel that the abuse was their fault or a reason for shame. They can see it was the result of sickness in the abuser. They can move through their anger to a place of inner peace and sometimes even compassion for their abuser. It is vital as well for the recovery of the abuser, and the prevention of any further abusive behavior, for perpetrators to tell their story, their whole story, and have it heard with understanding. It is our secrets, when we hide our story in shame and fear, that make us and keep us sick. We believe it is vital for everyone's healing in church and in society that these stories be told.

A third compelling reason for telling these stories is simply to humanize the perpetrator and break the cycle of abuse. In our experience one of the most damaging aspects of abuse is the objectification and dehumanization of both the victim and the abuser. The victim is treated like an object whose needs, emotions, and personhood are ignored and obscured or forcibly suppressed in the face of the abuser's sick "needs." The abuser dehumanizes himself by allowing the compulsive, offensive, abusive behavior to control him and suppress his own emotions, woundedness, rationality, values, and conscience. The very act of dehumanizing another person dehumanizes the self. A key part of our therapy with both victims and perpetrators is helping them rediscover and reempower all aspects of their humanity. For the perpetrators, this includes acknowledging and empathetically feeling their victims' humanity and pain.

Presenting the perpetrator as only a non-person, a less-than-human object of our horror, indignation, and scorn continues the dehumanizing cycle of abuse. For this reason, if for no other reason, the priest abuser's story needs to be told and listened to. The priest abuser needs to be seen and known as the human being he is in order for full healing to occur in victims and in perpetrators, in society, and in the Church. Only then will the cycle of abuse be fully broken.

Some will say that priest abusers do not deserve to have their stories told or heard. We certainly understand the emotions and pain behind this protestation. We in no way condone or excuse their abusive behaviors or the cover-up by some Church leaders. However, we firmly believe these stories need to be told for all of the reasons stated above and, finally, simply because of our shared humanity, simply because they are our brothers.

23

In the charged and adversarial atmosphere of the media and legal arenas, little is offered to show that healing must be the goal of all involved. There are few stories of either the victim or the abuser experiencing inner healing or much less stories of healing and reconciliation or forgiveness between abusers and victims. Healing is possible — we have seen it. We see it daily. Victims of abuse heal their wounds — although sometimes some scars of the abuse never fully heal — and move on to healthy and productive lives. Priest abusers, if they fully face their abusive behavior, have sorrow for their victims, heal their own wounds, and achieve ongoing recovery from their addictive, offending behaviors, can regain and live the vows and spirit of their priesthood, albeit in a new and limited way. This healing is rarely acknowledged or reported. Healing is happening beyond the headlines.

When a priest client has made sufficient progress in his recovery, we see a very psychologically and spiritually wounded man who deeply yearns for healing and wholeness. We feel blessed to work professionally with these men, to know the person beyond the abusive behavior. We have been blessed to see many of them experience substantial healing and ongoing recovery from their compulsive, offending sexual behavior. We have been greatly saddened in a few cases when recovery was not chosen.

COMPILING THE STORIES

A word about the process of putting these stories together. The five priests whose stories are presented in part one were invited to share their stories based on our extensive clinical experience with them. There were several criteria for their participation:

- Each had to be in full recovery from his sexual addiction and his sexually abusive behavior.

- Each had to have taken full responsibility for his sexually abusive behavior — no excuses or rationalizations.

- There could not be any personal agendas in their stories.

- They could not attempt to change their current situation or Church or public policy.

- They could not harbor secrets about past abusive behavior.

- Their stories had to omit any personally revealing or identifying details about themselves or their victims to ensure everyone's confidentiality and safety.

Part two presents three survivors' stories. We have chosen to present their stories second to illustrate, in sequence, the cycle of abuse, and the full process of healing. It also gives survivors the last word in the story of abuse. The process of involving victims, survivors of sexual abuse by clergy, was more informal. One of the survivors, on hearing about the book, eagerly volunteered to tell her story. Another survivor was invited. He was just as enthusiastic about participating. As the project unfolded, Sue Lauber-Fleming decided to openly tell her own personal story of abuse and healing. All were simply asked to write their story and describe their healing process, however they wanted to tell it. Our only criteria for the three survivor coauthors were that they be fairly advanced in their healing and that they keep their stories anonymous (except for Sue). Again, our purpose is to demonstrate the healing and hope that is possible for both priest perpetrators and victims of clergy abuse.

When we formed the idea to tell these stories, we realized it would be a very delicate project. We knew that it would be vital to protect the confidentiality and anonymity of counseling clients, both victims and priest perpetrators. Consequently, we insisted that the coauthors omit any identifying information about themselves or their victims in their stories.

We cannot verify the details of the stories told here. Nonetheless, we believe the stories are true in their essential content. In some cases, we have edited the stories to ensure confidentiality and readability. All of the stories are in the words of the priests and survivors themselves.

THE ROLE OF THE COMMENTARY

In part three, we present ideas for healing. This includes an approach for creating new stories about the abuse. These new narratives will help shape our perspectives about ourselves and about this issue — whether we are victims, perpetrators, or even the Church. Following that Mark Matousek tells about the residential facility he runs, which houses priests who no longer serve in active ministry for a variety of reasons. This amazing facility and its treatment programs have helped its residents reclaim their humanity and a new, albeit limited, place in the world.

Each story will be followed by a commentary by Patrick Fleming, providing a psychological and spiritual perspective. Each story has much to teach us. The commentaries elaborate on what created the horrible abusive cycle these individuals were caught up in and what helps to heal them, stop the abuse cycle, and prevent it from continuing.

A note about sexual orientation and abuse. Four of the five priests abused victims of the same gender. This is primarily an artifact of the population we are treating. There is no evidence that homosexual men as a group are any more likely to abuse than heterosexual men. In fact, the greatest preponderance of abuse is committed by heterosexual men.[3] In our experience the most common form of sexual abuse is father-daughter incest.

COMMITMENT TO HEALING

As you read these stories you may have a number of mixed and conflicting emotions: revulsion, nausea, anger or even rage, sadness, grief, compassion, and hope. You may even find yourself wanting to turn away from these stories. We understand all of these reactions, because, in the progression of our work first with victims and then with abusers, we have experienced all of them as well. We have been angry at the abuse along with our victim clients. We continue to hate what abusers have done to their victims. We hate the sickness that led them to abuse. However, as we began to work with the abusers, we found we could not hate them. As we heard their stories, sadness and compassion grew in us, as well as a profound sense of the wounded sacredness of their inner personhood.

Throughout our years of work with victims and abusers, the sustaining emotion and belief has been hope, hope that healing and recovery are possible for all.

We are simply telling the story behind the headlines, the tragic yet very human and ultimately hopeful story of the priest abuser and his victims. It is not our intention to write a professional therapy book. The heart of this book is the stories of the five priests and three victims we invited to participate. Though there are as many unique stories as there are victims and priests who have abused, we believe these eight stories will provide a new window into this human tragedy. In breaking their vows, these priests, these men, broke the hearts and trust of their victims, their Church, and themselves. This is their story of healing, abusers and victims, in their own words.

This project was born from our twenty years of professional experience working with victim-survivors of abuse, clerical sexual perpetrators, and Church leadership. We believe that within each of these groups there are profound, tragic human stories that need to be heard. We have helped our abuse survivor clients overcome their fear and their shame and tell their stories. We rejoice that they are finally receiving a hearing. We pray that this leads to healing for other victims and, in time, for the Church. We pray most of all that the process of opening this secret to the light will lead to effective prevention and protection for all our children.

Our goal is to bring healing. We hope that this message of hope and healing is disseminated as widely as possible. To this end, we decided that a portion of the profits from this endeavor would be contributed to healing for both victims and affected priests. Our commitment, and the commitment of the unnamed coauthors, is to donate a percentage of any profits to programs dedicated to bring healing: 25 percent will go to two programs for victims, the Restorative Justice Council on Sexual Misconduct in Faith Communities and the Healing Alliance (formerly known as Link-Up); and 25 percent will go to a fund for priests and brothers in need of recovery help. No proceeds from the book will go to the priest or survivor coauthors.

We pray, hope, and intend that this book, especially these stories by priest abusers and by victims of abuse, will be an instrument of healing this great and tragic wound for the individuals involved and for the Church itself.

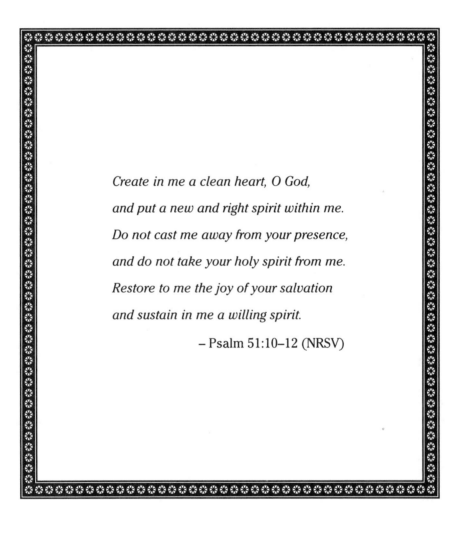

Create in me a clean heart, O God,

and put a new and right spirit within me.

Do not cast me away from your presence,

and do not take your holy spirit from me.

Restore to me the joy of your salvation

and sustain in me a willing spirit.

— Psalm 51:10–12 (NRSV)

THE HUMAN TRAGEDY
OF BROKEN TRUST

Two

A PRIEST
FROM THE DEEP SOUTH

My story is a story filled with trauma, sadness, joy, recovery, and hope. It is story of dreams shattered and dreams created, of hope lost and rediscovered. It is the story of a child of an alcoholic parent and a dysfunctional family system. It is a story that needs to be written and told in the hope that others may understand the truth of my humanity as a religious priest and perhaps once again discover the common human struggles and dreams that bind all of us together.

I was born in the Deep South in the early sixties as the youngest of six children. Two of my siblings died before my birth. My childhood was filled with chaos from my father's and two brothers' drinking. When they drank, they became verbally abusive toward my mother and me and sometimes physically abusive among themselves.

I distinctly remember two occasions before I was four when my mom was bathing me and my dad was heavily intoxicated. He was convinced that my mother was being unfaithful. He attempted to tear the bathroom door off its hinge with a loaded rifle in hand. I was fortunately able to escape, naked, through the open bathroom window to summon my aunt. She quickly rushed over to disarm him.

Days and nights were filled with arguments. On many such nights my mom would take me over to my aunt's house, where we both could find respite and rest from my father's behavior. My aunt's home became a safe haven from the raging storms of my father's and brothers' drunkenness. Sadly, it was at my aunt's house where I encountered my first and only incident of sexual abuse at the hands of my oldest brother.

My brother and I were alone. I was no more than four years old. He was approaching thirty. We were sitting next to each other. I recall that he was not drinking during this particular time. He reached over and began fondling my sexual organs through my clothes. Neither of us spoke while it was occurring. I somehow understood that this was to be a secret between us. I didn't feel afraid or threatened. I only remember that whatever was happening felt really pleasant. He fondled me for quite a few minutes. I never spoke of what happened between the two of us until much later in my life.

There are several reasons why I chose not to talk about it with my family at the time of my sexual abuse. First, I did not know I was the victim of abuse. Second, telling my mother and father would only have added to the pandemonium in my home. I was afraid to tell what had happened. My brother would certainly have vehemently denied my story.

The awareness of my sexual abuse dawned in my early adolescence. Like many victims of sexual molestation, I simply was not aware that I had been abused. Like many sexually violated children, I was filled with shame and confusion. I was also filled with many unanswered questions: Why did this happen? Was I to blame for what happened?

Why had my brother done this? What will happen if I tell someone? Who can I trust with this forbidden secret?

Soon after graduation from high school, I shared the story of my sexual abuse with my sister. She listened to my childhood story. She did not try to convince me that it had not happened. She heard and believed what my words and heart were saying. I have long since forgiven my oldest brother. Perhaps only he and God know what prompted him to sexually violate me so early in my life.

Although many of my memories from childhood and adolescence are unpleasant ones, happy memories also exist. I was not only the youngest, but also the smallest member of the family. I was born two months premature in the local hospital. Being small carried its privileges. I was constantly doted on by my mom. Although the family was poor, I had an overabundance of toys. Since I had no siblings close to my age, I learned to content myself with my large number of toys. Our family always had at least one dog in the home. I remember long happy hours of play with my toys and dogs. I love dogs as much now in my early forties as I did then in my childhood.

GROWING UP DIFFERENT

One of the most difficult parts of my childhood and adolescent years was my sexual orientation. I knew deep inside that I was gay from a very early age. However, sex was not an appropriate topic for discussion. After years of therapy it remains uncertain to what degree the sexual abuse from my older brother may have contributed to my sexual preference. I remember finding certain men attractive before the unfortunate sexual incident with my older brother. I do not believe that I am gay because another man sexually abused me. I believe one's sexual orientation is a result of social, environmental, and genetic factors, many of which are beyond one's control.

Growing up homosexual in a small town in a dysfunctional family during the 1970s was extraordinarily difficult. I couldn't talk about my sexual attraction to other males. Sex was seen as something dirty and nasty. My mom did not enjoy sex with my father. Usually my father was drinking when he began to harass and demand sex from my mother. Eventually she yielded to him in an attempt to satisfy and silence him. And so it was in this environment that I realized I was gay. I felt isolated physically, socially, and emotionally. Spiritually, the Catholic Church didn't seem to offer much solace because of its teachings against homosexuality. In many ways I was alone.

When I was eleven, a series of catastrophic events occurred. My favorite aunt, middle brother, and father all died within six months of each other. My aunt died of lung cancer. My brother drowned while at work offshore. My father committed suicide. I was left with my mom and alcoholic oldest brother in our home. I became my mom's confidante. Adult responsibilities were placed on my eleven-year-old, ninety-six-pound body.

My mom had lost a half-sister, a son, and a husband within six months. Her grief was tremendously intense. I was emotionally closest to my aunt. As cruel as it may sound to my readers, I was grateful for my father's and middle brother's deaths. The arguments between my father and mother were over. The cruelty suffered by the family dogs at the hands of my father and his namesake was ended. While I did feel some sadness at my father's passing, I grieved all the more because I hadn't had a father even while he was alive.

It seemed that my mom wept from sunrise into evening. I wept at the loss of my aunt. I loved her with a love that could not be described by words. She had become my second mother. She was a rock upon which my mother had leaned. I also wept because of my mom's sadness and loss. I began to masturbate during this time of emotional upheaval in our home. In the weeks and months of grief that followed, masturbation became a pleasant diversion and a coping mechanism. It afforded me a safe opportunity to fantasize about other males. When I masturbated I could daydream about being loved and accepted as young, small, and gay. I became compulsively addicted to my routine of masturbating in which I would fantasize and experience sexual pleasure from one to as much as five times daily.

ADULT ASPIRATIONS AND TEMPTATIONS

While many childhood dreams never materialized, I had one dream that I would not abandon. That dream was to be a priest. I didn't get to attend Mass often, mostly because of lack of family interest or transportation. I loved the silence, the reverence, and the safety from the emotional turmoil at home. My mom was the spiritual foundation of my family home. I remember waking many early mornings to find her sitting in front of the television praying the rosary in French along with the priest. She taught me how to pray. I've often remarked that my small family home was my first seminary. It was there that I learned about God. It was there that I first felt God. It was there that I first fell in love with God.

I graduated from high school at age nineteen. My brother presented me with a new car as a gift. Finally some freedom! I began college in the fall following my summer graduation, and I started to attend church often. I became very involved with the activities of the Newman Center on campus. I participated in retreats, workshops, and seminars. Whatever was happening, I could be counted on for help and participation. Unfortunately, church was not the only place I could be found.

During my college years, I lived with my brother. He had moved to the city several years before my high school graduation. We lived equally distant from the college campus and the college bars. It was during my freshman year of college that I started drinking on the weekends. At first I drank to know what it felt like to have alcohol inside me. Later I rationalized my weekend drinking by telling myself that I had earned a weekend of fun. I scored high marks in most of my classes; I didn't drink during the week; I continued to attend church regularly; I helped at the Newman Center as often as possible. I couldn't see any problems with my drinking.

My pattern of drinking changed during my junior year. I started barhopping during the weekdays. My studies began to be affected. Grades dropped. I was consuming too much alcohol, and I knew it. My mom cautioned me about my drinking as did my sister and brother. I decided to either stop drinking completely or drastically decrease my alcohol intake. I reverted to my pattern of weekends-only drinking at a more modest rate. My concentration improved and my grades soared. I began to feel emotionally and spiritually present when I was physically present at the Newman Center.

I had not forgotten my childhood dream of priesthood. My frequent presence at the Newman Center rekindled my childhood dream of becoming a priest. The pastor of the Center and my hometown pastor strongly encouraged me to consider the priesthood. Parishioners, friends, and college classmates suggested that I would be a natural fit for the priesthood.

I loved the Church immensely, although I was ill at ease with its teaching on homosexuality. I could not understand the sin involved in two people truly loving each other, especially if God was love. Guilt, fear, and shame prevented me from having sexual contact with others. Through my junior and senior year of college I prayed for a definite sign from God about priesthood.

I began corresponding with one of the vocation directors of a religious order in the Midwest. After two years of letters, phone calls, and personal visits, I decided to apply for candidacy. In January 1985 I was accepted as a candidate to begin my theological studies in Chicago in September of the same year following my college graduation.

After two years of studying theology as a candidate, I applied and was accepted into the novitiate. The novitiate is a yearlong process of spiritual preparation before professing vows of poverty, chastity, and obedience. I moved from Chicago to another large city. Four of us were received into the novitiate. We lived with two novice directors. The novitiate was undoubtedly one of the best spiritual years of my life. We learned the history of our religious congregation as well as key concepts in our spirituality. It was the only time in all of my religious training, formation, and years of ordained ministry that I felt loved, understood, and accepted.

I first shared my homosexual preference with my brothers in my novitiate year. I shared my yearnings and my struggles. I shared my heart's desire to be a religious and priest. My religious brothers, including my directors, assured me of their understanding and support. Yet the question remained deep inside: how can I truly embrace chastity if I've never experienced sex with another?

In January 1988 I was working as a student chaplain in an inner-city hospital. We were asked to volunteer and minister for at least eight hours per week while in novitiate. I met a very attractive young man in his early twenties at the hospital. We were immediately attracted sexually to each other. We exchanged phone numbers and within a few days became sexually involved with each other.

That first experience of gay sex left me feeling excited, afraid, and confused. I felt torn between this nice attractive man and religious life. He was my first sexual love. I spoke openly to my novice directors and my other religious brothers. I sought the advice of my spiritual director and confessor. And I prayed. During the course of several weeks, I realized that my love for the religious life and ministry was greater than my feelings from my first sexual love. I ended all communication and contact with him approximately two months after we had first met.

At the end of my novitiate, I professed temporary vows and returned to Chicago to continue theology studies. During the first two years of theology, I drank moderately. I continued to drink in my third and fourth year of studies. I began to drink not only in the seminary building proper, but also in several gay clubs. I was able to restrain myself from any sexual activity with others until after ordination.

40

LOSING CONTROL

My addiction to alcohol and sex became terribly fierce after graduation from seminary. I was assigned to a large city in the Southwest as part of immediate preparation for final vows and ordination. I spoke Spanish fluently and worked for several years in large Hispanic parishes. I began to frequent the gay district and to solicit anonymous sex with other adult males. In addition to the daily masturbation since age eleven, I was now using sex with others along with alcohol to relieve stress, to fit into the gay scene, and to cope with feelings of fatigue and social isolation.

I remember one particular weekend. I had recently celebrated a Mass of healing which many parishioners enjoyed immensely. As I was taking my liturgical vestments off, I noticed my hands were shaking and I was sweating profusely. The shakes! I needed a drink to steady my nerves and calm my movements. As I was drinking my rather large martini upstairs, I was watching the parishioners laugh and socialize before leaving in their cars. I yearned to feel their happiness and peace. I believed that God had worked through me to touch them with a measure of joy and healing. Yet I was the one filled with endless sadness and conflict with an eight-ounce glass of gin in hand.

My alcohol intake progressed from daily evening drinking for about eighteen months to drinking throughout the day for approximately the last six months before my first intervention. I could not function without alcohol. I needed quite a few ounces of gin to prevent my hands from shaking in the morning. My appearance at bars and clubs began to increase from occasional weekends to nearly every weekend. I was becoming increasingly more sexually promiscuous.

Every month resulted in fifteen to twenty different sexual partners. My life consisted of work, alcohol, sex, and sleep. This unbroken cycle remained constant for nearly two years. It was during these years that both my oldest brother and my mother died.

My oldest brother died approximately seven months before my mother passed away. He collapsed from a heart attack in his home. While he and I had never enjoyed close emotional ties, my mother was stricken once again by the grief of death. She had survived to bury four of her six children. She would not be able to weather the loss of her firstborn child in light of her ongoing medical problems with emphysema and congestive heart failure. My brother's death would simply be too much for her malfunctioning heart to bear. My sister and I were both clearly aware of the impending consequences of our brother's death on our mother's health.

My alcohol abuse intensified after my mother's death when I was thirty-three. Immediately after her death, my work schedule changed drastically. I would drink at least several ounces of gin after awakening in order to celebrate the liturgy and eat breakfast. More gin would be consumed after breakfast. I accepted only appointments or marriage preparation and the celebration of funerals. The time between appointments found me drinking upstairs in my study. I could no longer maintain a normal work schedule. The less I worked, the more I drank. As I drank I continued to sexually act out with anonymous men.

I wanted to stop drinking and having sex, but I could not do so by my own willpower. I was ashamed and afraid to ask for help. I did not want to be taken out of ministry. My drinking and sexual behavior seemingly had once been my solution. Now they had become my greatest adversaries.

I was oblivious to the abuse caused by my drinking and inappropriate sexual behavior. I could possibly concede that I was harming myself physically, psychologically, and spiritually. But while I was caught in the storm of my addictions, I truly did not believe that anyone else was suffering abuse from my drinking and sexual actions. The potential harm my intoxicated driving posed to the life and health of other drivers did not serve as a deterrent or cause for self-alarm. I convinced myself that I drove more safely while drinking than many others around me drove while sober. As ridiculous as I now realize my thoughts were then, I was trapped in the insane thinking patterns of my addictions.

Nor could I believe that my sexual behavior with other consenting males was damaging to them. I readily agreed with my therapist that my sexual behavior was the cause of my tremendous spiritual and emotional conflict. But I could not understand how engaging in sexual acts with other consenting adult males was abusive. After all, we both wanted sex with each other. I did not force alcohol or sex upon them. The seduction, lies, and manipulations were all part of the game. I justified my sexual activities by telling myself that I was human. I needed to express my sexuality. I was clearly aware that I was violating my vow of chastity. I consoled myself with the thought that chastity was an ideal that I could not be humanly expected to attain. If anyone was a victim, it was certainly I! How could anyone truly believe that refraining from all sexual activity with self or others was a healthy choice?

I also knew that my drinking was out of control. I rationalized my drinking by telling myself that if anyone else had lived through all the chaos and the many deaths of relatives in my childhood and adolescence, they most likely would also have turned to the bottle. It was indeed a wonder that I had not begun drinking much earlier! Poor me! Oh, I think I'll pour me another drink!

Celebrating Mass and other religious ceremonies became perfunctory. It was simply a job for which I earned money, money which I used for more liquor and the cover charge at different gay bars, money with which I bought food and other items for the many men with whom I had sexual contact.

Realizing how out of control I was, my sister took the initiative and called my provincial superior. He phoned me and requested that I cease all driving and withdraw from all liturgical celebrations until I completed a complete psychological assessment and treatment for alcoholism and depression.

EMBRACING RECOVERY

As I began my recovery, I began to realize more clearly the impact of my addiction to alcohol and sex on myself and others. I was perhaps the one person most psychologically and spiritually damaged. While I no longer felt comfortable wearing clerical clothes, I needed to continue to do so, for they provided me with an identity and a role without which I would be lost. I was my work. My work defined me and gave me purpose and meaning. I was a man in his early thirties without self-awareness. I did not know or love the real me. Although I had preached and taught about God's love, I had never personally felt loved and accepted by God. Once I embraced recovery and the spirituality of the Twelve Steps of Alcoholics Anonymous, my spiritual well-being and mental clarity returned.

My awareness of the impact of the abuse I caused continues to deepen. My relatives, especially my mother and sister, were filled with anxiety and sadness as my alcoholism progressed. My parishioners were also affected since I was not truly present with them. I had jeopardized the safety of thousands by driving while intoxicated. I had sexually exploited married men as well as others engaged to be married.

I had exposed myself and others countless times to the possibility of HIV and AIDS. I realized that I had been objectifying men. They had become objects of pleasure through which I found immediate sexual gratification. I learned that regardless of the form, addictions always leave victims in their path of destruction.

Over the years, I have been placed in at least a dozen different treatment centers across the country. I've been diagnosed with bipolar disorder and have been taking appropriate medications for more than four years. My current provincial superior and I both agree that public, sacramental ministry is no longer a viable option in my future because of my frequent relapses into alcohol and sexual activity.

Once while on a trip to Europe I relapsed after more than three years of sobriety. While I was counseling a twenty-three-year-old man in confession, I placed my hand on his thigh. He contacted the bishop of the diocese where I was assigned. I was immediately removed from all public ministries.

I realize now that I sexually violated this young adult man. He sought my professional assistance and I betrayed his trust. I believe that my actions have left him with difficulty in trusting others, especially other males and priests. My sexual violation has also resulted in feelings of anger, disappointment, embarrassment, and perhaps even shame in my victim. I am truly sorry for the harm I have caused to him and to everyone else while I was drinking and sexually acting out. I have made amends wherever possible. My best amends to others and myself is to maintain my sobriety.

Public ministry is no longer a viable option for me also because my spirituality has drastically changed over the years. I am no longer in agreement with some of the Church's teachings and policies. I could not return to ordained ministry in good conscience even if I were offered the opportunity. I would not jeopardize the integrity of my sobriety by preaching and teaching what I no longer believe in conscience.

These days find me wearing blue jeans, casual shirts, and cowboy boots. I live in the countryside surrounded by woods and ponds. I've grown a mustache and goatee. I attend two or three AA meetings a week and meet with my therapist once a week. I participate in group therapy once a week. I stay in close touch with my sponsor. Later this year I will begin the formal process of seeking laicization from religious life and the priesthood.

The foundation of my spirituality rests in the Twelve Steps of Alcoholics Anonymous. I have also been integrating some Native American and Buddhist spirituality into my Christian formation. For the first time in my life, I am at peace with myself and with my Higher Power. I clearly see God's beauty in all of life and in all of nature. If God is at all, God is for all and in all. I am content to be of service to others around me, to love and spoil my three dogs and three turtles, and to sit and feed the Canada geese that visit occasionally.

My prayer life is simple. Each morning I ask my Higher Power to help me remain sober. I ask that his will be done always. Before falling asleep each evening, I thank my Higher Power for another day of sobriety. I ask only that his will continue to be done. I thank God for my sobriety, my family, the love and generosity of my religious community, my AA sponsor, and my three dogs.

While the future seems uncertain, and the path is certainly sometimes difficult, I am looking forward to pursuing a graduate degree in either counseling or social work. I want to share my experience, strength, and hope with others like myself. While a long-term romantic relationship is not in my immediate future, I do wish to have that option remain open as the future continues to unfold. While I have not consciously chosen to be homosexual, I would not choose to be different even if the opportunity presented itself.

I am sometimes asked whether I am disappointed or bitter with the Church. While I find myself in strong disagreement with some of the Church's teachings, I cannot fault my religious community in their care and concern for my recovery and well-being. They have done everything possible to help me and have afforded me every possible opportunity to remain in ministry. They could not do what I most needed to do for myself. My provincial superiors have sometimes strongly confronted me because of my past dishonesty and unwillingness to live in recovery and remain sober. I have never doubted their love and care. As they have often assured me, they only want a healthy and productive future for me.

My story is a story in process as the future continues to unfold. It is ultimately a story of gratitude, hope, and serenity. It is a story of triumph over tremendous obstacles, of hope over despair, and of dreams once shattered and abandoned replaced with new dreams now discovered and claimed. It is the story of a child of a very dysfunctional home. It is the story of a child of God.

Ψ COMMENTARY

Although this story does not involve sexual abuse by a priest of a minor, since all of the sexual partners or victims are adults, it does dramatically illustrate many of the dynamics involved in the sexual abuse scandal in the Church. The author vividly recounts the abuse and trauma he suffered as a child in a very addicted, abusive, and dysfunctional family. We can see in his story the trauma which, unhealed, became the seed for his later multiple addictions leading eventually to his abusive behavior. This trauma was compounded by the extreme inner conflict and shame of growing up homosexual in a family, Church, and rural social environment that shamed anyone with that orientation. His early sexual abuse at the hands of his brother further added to his sexual confusion, secrecy, and shame.

Victims and Abusers Who Were Victims

Because victims and abusers are usually both victims and share the same deeply wounding trauma, they have many symptoms in common. One of the most damaging of these common symptoms is toxic shame. John Bradshaw defines shame as "the feeling of being flawed and diminished and never measuring up....With toxic shame there's something wrong with you and there is nothing you can do about it; you are inadequate and defective. Toxic shame is the core of the wounded child."[4]

Such shame is profoundly debilitating. The belief that one is fundamentally bad, defective, and worthless colors all that a person perceives, feels, and does. Victims' shame, created by the sexual abuse, causes them to turn their anger about the abuse onto themselves. They hate themselves and feel worthless. Their shame-based self-hate leads them to reject their bodies, their sexuality, and many aspects of themselves. This greatly affects their relationships and how they function in the world. It is also the basis for a victim's depression and tendencies toward self-harm.

It affects them spiritually as well. Victims often feel that, since they are so bad, God could not possibly love or accept them. Often this results in feeling rejected by or alienated from God, disrupting their spiritual relationship. This is especially true for victims of clerical sexual abuse. Because they have been sexually abused by a priest, they feel that they must be especially bad. It is difficult to reclaim their trust in God, since their trust has been betrayed by someone who is supposed to lead them to God.

Abusers, who are usually also victims of abuse, suffer from especially severe shame. Besides their original toxic shame from their own victimization, they feel overwhelming shame about having abused others. Compensatory narcissism, self-entitlement, and rationalization of their behavior may mask this shame. With victims, shame is manifested as self-directed anger. In unrecovered victim-abusers, abusers who were once victims of sexual abuse themselves, the self-anger is directed at both the self and also outwardly at others. This is part of the dynamic that leads them to abuse others. The common denominator for both victim and victim-abuser is the shame-based self-anger or hate. For the victims, this leads them mostly to be abusive to themselves. With the victim-abuser, shame drives them to be abusive to themselves and to their victims. This is one of the primary differences between victims and victim-abusers.

In addition to shame, victims and abusers share similar patterns in their difficulty with relationships. They find it difficult to trust others and consequently difficult to get close. Their very poor opinion of themselves keeps them from believing others could love or enjoy them. They fear betrayal, abandonment, or being engulfed by another. They end up feeling socially different, isolated, and believe they do not fit in anywhere.

Their tendency to depression and high levels of anxiety is also comparable. Victims feel helpless in the face of the abuser's greater power, either physical or psychological. This feeling of helplessness, if untreated, can endure throughout life, creating a feeling of constant vulnerability leading to chronic anxiety. The world feels to the abused like a perpetually dangerous place. The victim-abuser feels equally helpless and fearful, although this is often covered up by acting as if he felt powerful. The victim-abuser feels both helpless and powerful as he engages in his compulsive, offending, abusive behavior.

Both groups may be driven to various addictions, as we see in this man's story, in an attempt to anesthetize their pain. Alcoholism, drug addiction, sex and love addiction, or compulsive avoidance of sex (sometimes called sexual anorexia), compulsive overeating or other eating disorders, compulsive self-cutting, codependency, gambling, and other addictions frequently develop. It is ironic and tragic that the pain of being abused leads some victims to develop a sexual addiction or compulsion that in some cases leads to sexually abusive behavior, which creates more victims. This is the cycle of abuse that must end.

Many victims and victim-abusers learn to dissociate, mentally distancing themselves from the pain and events of the abuse. It is an experience of feeling numb, out of one's body, disconnected to what did happen or is happening to them now. This is linked to a generalized inability to feel any of their emotions, except sometimes anger and intense fear. Repetition compulsion, another aspect of dissociating, is the tendency to unconsciously seek out and repeat some aspect of the original abuse trauma. It is an unconscious attempt to heal or overcome the original trauma. In victims, for instance, this can lead to compulsively seeking out people or situations, even in their adult life, that are in some way abusive.[5]

For the victim-abuser, the interaction of repetition compulsion, dissociation, and emotional repression helps to create a pattern of compulsive sexual behavior, some of which becomes abusive to others. The dissociation and lack of emotion prevents the abuser from feeling the impact of his abusive behavior on his victim. The capacity for empathy, which enables us to feel the effect of our behavior on another, has been impaired by abuse. He cannot feel the effect of his own victimization, and he cannot feel what he is doing to his victims. For instance, this man rationalized that he was not hurting anyone by his sexual actions when his sexual addiction was out of control. Treatment for victim-abusers includes helping them feel the pain of their own abuse and helping them feel the pain they have caused their victims.

You can see clearly in this brief summary of the common symptoms and struggles of both the victim and the abuser that their plight is very similar and inextricably intertwined. These are not two distinct classes of people, one deserving our sympathy, the other our condemnation. They are both wounded and psychologically sickened in very similar ways and by the same original trauma. They are both caught up in the tragic cycle of abuse. In order to break the cycle of abuse, we need to see these perpetrators, without ever excusing their behavior, as the wounded, victimized human beings that they are, sharing the same story and the same humanity as their victims.

This man's family and social situation provided him with few resources to handle all of his pain, shame, and fear. So it is not surprising to see him begin to medicate his pain sexually with compulsive masturbation at the age of eleven. This is when his world further fell apart with the deaths of his aunt, father, and brother in a short time. His mother, who with his aunt had been his emotional lodestone, sank into depression at her losses. The sexual self-soothing that he employed started a process that resulted in a full-blown sexual addiction by the time he was in his late twenties and was an ordained priest.

The progression and interaction of his addictions — alcoholism and sex addiction — is painfully clear. His alcoholism, his primary addiction, to which he is most likely genetically predisposed, began in college and greatly accelerated after ordination. The accelerant seems to have been a combination of the pressure of a very high workload, unresolved childhood pain, and the shame of his sexually addicted behavior, which in turn was fueled by his drinking. His workaholism was driven by this shame and his childhood role of caretaker and peacemaker. The vicious circles that he was caught up in eventually spiraled out of control.

A Cleric's Life

This is a frequent pattern for many clergy, not just those who sexually act out or abuse. Parishioners typically do not think that priests ever need a day off. This is an assumption, from parishioners and from themselves, that drives clergy of all faiths. There is an expectation of continual sacrificial ministry with little or no time for self-care, self-growth, or self-discovery. Too often there is also an inadequate support system for the clergy. Who do priests, ministers, or rabbis turn to when they are in need? I once inadvertently provoked a full-blown panic attack in an overworked Protestant minister whom I was counseling when I merely suggested he begin to look at some of his personal needs!

When the pattern of work addiction so common in clergy is not faced, this feeds other addictions. Alcoholism or the abuse of drugs are among the most frequent. Unfortunately, sexual addiction resulting in various types of inappropriate sexual behavior is also a possibility for the overextended clergyman or clergywoman. The addictions to alcohol, sex, and work interact, feeding upon each other in a vicious downward spiral.

There is also a progression in loss of control and crossing of boundaries in violation of one's values and beliefs. As this man's drinking increased, his sexual addiction progressed to more and more compulsive sexual encounters in violation of his vow of celibacy. These increasingly were anonymous and objectifying of the other and self. With the death of his oldest brother and beloved mother, his addictions increased further to numb the pain he felt at their loss. The thought distortions that accompany all addictions became more predominant. He rationalized and denied to himself the reality and impact of his addictions on himself and others, a prime example of the blindness of addiction. This is all part of the eventual total deterioration of the person under the power of an addiction or multiple addictions.

It is difficult for anyone who has not been caught up in the sickness and insanity of an addiction to understand how this could happen to a man such as this one. This is part of what makes it so incomprehensible to most that a priest could end up sexually abusing a child. But to anyone who has been caught in the throes of addiction, or has known an active, out-of-control addict, it is sadly too understandable how an addiction can lead the addict — priest or not — to behaviors that are otherwise incomprehensible and even abusive of others. Addictions progressively take over and distort people, their thought processes, their conscience, their values, their spirituality, their boundaries, and their behavior. The addiction hijacks their brain, their whole personhood.

This is what happened to this man. Thankfully, we can also see in his story the hope of recovery. His distorted thinking cleared. He sees and accepts the damage he did to others and to himself. He feels great sorrow and empathy for his victims. He sees how he was using his sexual partners or victims in his sexual addiction as "objects of pleasure" rather than treating them as fellow human beings. You can sense the peace that he is achieving with himself, despite the loss of his priesthood, in his acceptance of the consequences of his addictions, in his ease with himself, and in his simple life lived close to nature. His words depict a growing and more personal spirituality. Most of all, he finally has achieved sobriety, serenity, and relative freedom from the oppression of his addictions.

Three

A PRIEST
AND HIS FATHER

~~~~~~~~~~~~~~~~~

I am a suspended, inactive priest in my late seventies. One of the strongest memories of my childhood is of a day when I was around seven years old. I had just graduated from first grade, and I remember going through the dark cloakroom in the back of the classroom. I had a report card for the year, which was very poor. I was afraid to show that report card to my parents, especially my father. It took me a full hour to walk home, even though my house was only a block away! When I finally got home, my mother quickly signed the report card, and I ran it back to the school so my father wouldn't see it.

I lived in considerable fear of my father. He was very harsh and tough. For instance, if I lost a fight with a neighbor boy, my father would take me back and make me beat that child. Oh, how I hated that; those boys were my friends! But to please my father and win his affection, I had to hurt my friends. I only received my father's approval if I was tough like him and a good fighter.

My mother was in many ways at the other extreme. I resented this just as much. She spoiled me, yet her affection seemed stilted and artificial. I felt accepted by her only when I fit a certain image of what she thought I was, not by being

56

who I really was. She frequently embarrassed me in public as a child. She would tell others I was "a very fine boy, a good moral boy." However, I realized I was not the perfect boy she represented me to be. Later, in my senior year of high school, she bought me a golden football for my school coat when I had played only ten minutes all year and was the only one on the team whose parents could afford such a display.

With Mom, I always felt a pressure to be something more than I was. Her love felt conditional upon her high expectations of me, including her goal for me to become a priest. When I was twelve, she intercepted a letter I was sending to a girl I had a crush on. She wouldn't let me send it and told me it would interfere with plans to pursue becoming a priest.

YOUNG AND ALONE

My childhood had changed dramatically when I was ten years old. My mother went to work full-time in my father's office. They both worked long hours. This meant that I generally did not see them till late at night. I hated the fact that my mother was not at home with me. I resented that she was not there when I emotionally needed her presence to support me. We lived in a seemingly safe, small town, but I was scared to be alone so frequently. One Saturday night when I was ten, I had gone to a movie by myself, which I often did. It was a scary, spooky movie. After the movie was over, I ran home in the dark as fast as I could. I came home to an empty house; Mom was not there. I was terrified and bitterly resented that my mother was not home to comfort me.

One day when I was eleven, I was once again home alone, my parents at work. A neighborhood high school boy came to the house and forced me to engage in mutual masturbation. In the course of the masturbation, the older boy put his ejaculation on my penis. I developed an infection in my penis, which lasted for some time. I feared to tell my parents and feared the boy if I said anything. I was also deeply ashamed of myself. I never told anyone about this boy abusing me until this year when I told the other men and my therapist in my therapy group.

Following this incident, I developed a habit of frequent, compulsive masturbation. I felt very bad that I did this, but I could not stop it. Once when I was thirteen, I was home alone and masturbating. My mother unexpectedly came home and caught me. I was deeply embarrassed. She proceeded to give me a sex talk. As part of this, she told me about my uncle who had gotten syphilis from the town prostitute, which led to his death. That summer we went to Washington, D.C., and visited the Smithsonian Institution. In the medical section I saw horrible, graphic pictures of the effect syphilis had on the body; in one you could see the person's skin eaten away to reveal the intestines. All of this had a very strong effect on me. I became very fearful of sex and of being infected with a sexual disease. Yet I could not stop masturbating.

My parents continued to work together weekdays till quite late. I rarely saw either my father or my mother. This situation existed until my junior or senior year of high school, when my parents divorced as a result of an affair my father was having with his secretary. I moved with my mother to another town.

A PRIEST ALONE

I went to one year of college, but World War II had broken out, so I dropped out and joined the navy. I saw a lot of action aboard ship and was in five major battles. I witnessed the deaths of several friends whom I cared about. Afterward, nightmares greatly disturbed my sleep for the first five years following my service. Like most veterans, I never told anyone of my nightmares or what I had experienced in combat. After all, I was supposed to be tough like my father.

When I left the navy after the war, I entered a seminary to study to become a priest like many other Catholic veterans affected by the war. You might say that fear of the bullet drove me into the priesthood. Classes at the seminary were very hard for me. I often thought of myself as stupid. I worked and worked to make it through the studies, leaving little time for relaxation or friends, so I had few friends. It was a hard and lonely road through the seminary.

But I made it. I was ordained a Catholic priest and was assigned to a parish with a school. For seven years I was just an ordinary, good parish priest. Yet inside I thought very poorly of myself. I felt ashamed that I continued to struggle with masturbation. It is hard to describe what it was like to live with this. I hated myself for it, but the masturbation, often two to three times a day, would accomplish what nothing else could do. It made me temporarily feel good inside, and then fairly quickly I felt awful again. I would make an inner vow to stop. But the urge would be so strong and compelling that, if I didn't give in, I would have a pointless and useless day because I was so preoccupied by it. A few years after ordination my doctor told me to stop smoking. When I did I became very depressed and anxious. That just increased the frequency of temptation and the power that masturbation had over me.

I felt myself to be much less competent than my fellow priests. I went to meetings with other priests and wanted to add my thoughts to whatever was being discussed, but I couldn't. I became so fearful of saying something stupid and looking like a fool that I could rarely bring myself to say anything. I went away from those meetings so angry for not being able to speak that I wanted to destroy someone, including myself. I was unable to express what I knew to be truthful and honest or to offer my opinion. I would think it, but never could I say it. As a consequence of my inability to participate, everyone regarded me as a nincompoop and a little boy, which I was.

I tried to be a good parish priest the first years of my priest-hood, and I suppose I mostly did so despite my problems. Yet I felt so empty emotionally, empty like my childhood home. I believe my mother's absence when I needed consolation and encouragement left me with a lack of emotional strength and courage to do the things I needed to do as an adult. This kept me from feeling for people the way I thought that I should as a priest. I cared about my parishioners, but I could not feel their joy or their pain. I remember sadly one occasion when a woman came to see me for help after she had survived a serious accident. I tried, but I could feel no compassion for her. I felt she went away even more distressed and also dissatisfied with me.

UNABLE TO PRAY

After seven years as a parish priest, my bishop asked me to go away to school to get a graduate degree in psychology because he wanted me to become a chaplain for a mental hospital. I requested not to, but the bishop said I was the only one available. So I went.

To obtain my degree, I chose to write a thesis on psychopathic personalities. The research for my thesis led me into material that included pornography, some of this pertaining to the sexual abuse of children. Some was very graphic and was very harmful to me. My mind became flooded with these images and sick thoughts. They would appear especially when I masturbated, which I continued to do often despite my attempts to quit. I shut down spiritually. I stopped praying my daily Office (psalms, scripture readings, and other prayers required of a priest at different times of the day). I stopped praying the rosary. In fact, I just didn't pray, period.

I was in a very bad state when I returned to my diocese and began to serve as a chaplain in a mental institution for a couple of years. It was when I was sent to a parish that I began to sexually abuse girls. My victims were girls from eight to about fifteen or sixteen. My abuse mostly took the form of touching them genitally, in a few cases attempting intercourse with them. I knew what I was doing was wrong, but I seemed to be unable to do anything about it. I could not stop myself, just like it had always been with my masturbating. I felt myself to be very evil and very empty, and I was desolate emotionally and spiritually. I was doing horrible things to these innocent young girls, and I could not stop myself.

Even when I was moved to a different parish or a different town, I could not stop. I was tormented by my obsession and knew I was hurting these girls, yet there seemed to be no cure. A part of me wanted to stop my abusing, but it was not strong enough to overcome my almost demonic compulsion

61

to abuse. The small part of me that was still healthy wanted to be caught in my crimes, because that seemed to be the only way I could stop hurting people. This, I believe, was unconsciously behind my behavior at a hospital where I was chaplain: I crawled into bed with a disabled woman in her thirties and attempted to rape her. A nurse easily caught me, and I was arrested.

I pleaded guilty and was sentenced to three months of "shock" imprisonment. I worked in the prison chapel. Each day I worked to scrape many years' layers of wax from the floor with a single-blade razor on the end of a long pole. This was followed by one month in a prison mental hospital for evaluation. I received no treatment there. I was then re-leased on three years probation and saw a psychiatrist for one year, fifteen minutes each week.

I was able to stop and control my impulses to abuse young girls after prison. I never abused or was sexual with a minor again. That was twenty-six years ago. My main motivation, honestly, was fear; inside, I was still sick. My time in prison had taught me that if I ever abused again, this or worse would happen to me. The "shock" of prison worked.

Yet, my addiction to sex continued. I was still masturbat-ing twice a day, always twice a day. I could not stop. I was still dead spiritually, and I was full of self-hate for what I had done to those girls. Despite this, I returned to pastoral work as a priest. I bounced around. I worked in a parish for a while, and then I did missionary work in Latin America. I loved the work and the people there and did not abuse anyone, yet the compulsive lust was like a monkey on my back, always gnawing on me. I could not shake it off. I was consumed by it and had not a moment's peace.

I connected with a religious order and went to Africa as a missionary hoping to find relief there. I again loved the work and the people, but the sex addiction would not leave me. I hoped to die there in that poor country, and the sooner the better! I did get very sick and had to return to the States for medical treatment. I recovered and eventually was helping out in a parish in a U.S. diocese.

IN THE COMPANY OF OTHERS

Then around thirteen or fourteen years ago, two events occurred that finally brought me relief. The first came in the form of a letter from the bishop of my original diocese where most of my abusive behavior had occurred. One of my victims, now an adult woman, had written to him saying that because of my behavior, I should not be allowed to say Mass. I agreed with her. I immediately wrote the bishop requesting that my faculties to publicly function as a priest be revoked. I was no longer an active priest. This had a profound and strangely positive effect on me, which I still cannot entirely explain. It felt like a huge weight had been lifted from me. I no longer had to try to be something outwardly that I did not feel myself worthy to be inwardly. The pressure to prove myself as a priest that had started with my mother was no longer there. The compulsive masturbation spontaneously ceased.

Very soon after this I met a priest who became my confessor and spiritual director. He was a godsend. He led me back to prayer. He told me to pray constantly through the day. I returned to praying the Office, memorizing much of it so it would be easier to pray. He also taught me to constantly guard myself about what I saw, heard, or said to prevent my mind from being filled again with sexual thoughts. My hearing, speech, eyes, and heart finally became clear of all the sexual garbage and filth I had been obsessed with for so many years. The monkey was finally off my back. I never masturbated again. I stopped fantasizing sexually, although I continued at times to be tormented with sexual dreams (these stopped completely only recently). I was at last spiritually alive and truly celibate, even though now not living or ministering as a priest.

For the next thirteen years I lived very simply and anonymously. I lived alone in a small camper trailer. It was a life of bare subsistence at times, and I was very much alone. I would live six months in one area of the country and then move for six months to a warmer area of the country and then back to the first area. Whenever I could, I worked in a soup kitchen as an unpaid volunteer serving food to the poor. I did not disclose that I was a priest or anything about the abuse that I had committed. I was afraid I might not be allowed to work. I did not function as a priest at all during this time. I saw this time as a life of prayer, service, and penance for what I had done to my victims. I developed a lifestyle that worked for me, although it was quite spare and empty of relationships. I continued to have no difficulties sexually. The prayer and the work at the soup kitchens were my chief consolations.

During the latter years of this period, I met with, talked with, or corresponded with a few of my victims, now all adult women. This was at their initiative. I felt that perhaps in talking to them, expressing my apologies — although my words always felt thin and inadequate in light of the enormity of what I had done to them — listening to their pain or anger and answering whatever questions they had about the

64

abuse, I could help a little in their healing. On a couple of occasions, I met with the victim and the new bishop of my old diocese to help the victim heal. The bishop was very solicitous about these victims' needs and felt that my presence would help them. These contacts with my victims were very difficult for me and brought up much pain and guilt. Some seemed more successful than others. My hope is that they brought some healing to the horrible hurt I caused these women when they were girls.

A couple of years ago some of the victims came out publicly with the story of what I had done to them. The media contacted me, and I told them my story as well. This made it impossible for me to continue my life as it had been for thirteen years. I could no longer work in the soup kitchens. My few acquaintances mostly would no longer abide my presence. I began to feel harassed by a couple of my victims and by the media, feeling they were out to destroy me. It did not seem to matter that I had changed my life so much for the better. I felt angry that I was losing the life that had worked so well for me, peculiar as it was. Yet I believed, and sometimes still believe, that I deserved anything I got because of what I did to these innocent girls.

At that point, my bishop told me he wanted me to move to a new situation, my current residential program, where I would be supervised and cared for. I am happy for it. I was at first reluctant to go, and I do still miss the freedom I had in those last years. Yet the time here has been good for me. In therapy, I have found out the reason why I am and was the way I was. I enjoy the company of other priests and brothers who understand me because they have had similar problems. I feel accepted and secure. The time I have and the atmosphere here have allowed me to perfect myself in the spiritual life.

The last fourteen years, and especially in therapy this last year here in this program, have allowed me to piece together what happened in my life and what caused me to inflict such horrible hurt. When I stopped masturbating I had to face this issue. What I had been doing all these years was a sign of immaturity, reflecting an inability to grow and become a person able to enjoy the company of others. Now I feel able to be at least some of what I always should have been. I am sexually celibate. My prayer life is active, and I am again trying to grow spiritually. I enjoy talking to, joking with, and praying with the men I live with. I count a few of them as real friends, something I never knew before.

I live with guilt and regret that are beyond words to express about what I did to those young girls I abused. This weighs upon me daily. I pray for my victims each day that they might be able to overcome the damage that I did to them and live happy lives. I feel very guilty for the moral damage I have caused the Church, especially my diocese, and the financial damage I have caused them as well. I feel such a desperate frustration that there is little I can do to make up for my behavior. So I pray; that is all I know to do.

Despite all of this, these days I find increasing peace inside. My life here is simple. I no longer feel so alone. I feel the residents and staff here understand and accept me. Piecing together the events of my life and seeing how my awful problems developed has lessened my hate for myself. I find moments of peace in prayer, in my daily exercise, in my simple diet, in small chats with fellow residents. I am not tormented with constant lust. I am free of that at last. I can voice my opinions and share some of my struggles and be a friend and a part of a community. Perhaps, finally this late in life, I am growing up to be a little of what I wanted to be and God wanted me to be all of these years.

Ψ COMMENTARY

This is an incredibly disturbing, haunting, tragic, yet ultimately hopeful story of a journey to the eventual healing and freedom of a deeply wounded soul. I know this man as a kind, gentle, humble, and deeply spiritual elderly priest, which contrasts so greatly with the severity of the abuse he inflicted on his child victims. It is very disturbing, of course, to read of the abuse he inflicted in his sickness upon his innocent young victims. It is perhaps even more upsetting to realize that little was done to stop his abusing behavior by his then bishop (who is now deceased). This man wanted to be stopped, could not stop himself, but eventually found a way to be caught and stopped. So much suffering for his victims and for himself might have been prevented. It is hard to fathom why his bishop failed to intervene, protect the children, and get this man the professional help he needed. It is also hard to understand why the criminal justice system and the mental health professionals involved did not ensure better monitoring and psychological help for this troubled man.

The Cycle of Abuse

This is a haunting, tragic story because, in retrospect, we can see how the traumatically wounding events of his childhood set him up to eventually become an abuser. As happens too often, the abused, wounded child grows into an adult who wounds and abuses. The emotional abandonment by his parents, leaving him alone frequently, their pressure for him either to be tough or to be good beyond reason, left him, by ten years of age, with considerable internal anger, emotional emptiness, and low self-esteem. Being sexually abused by a teenage boy, at age eleven, compounded his internal shame, anger, and aloneness. This led to a pattern of fear, shame, and obsession about sex combined with sexual self-soothing which progressed to compulsive, addictive sexual behavior and to his eventual abuse of young girls. The cycle of abuse is very apparent here. As William Wordsworth wrote, "The Child is father of the Man."[6] When the child has been profoundly traumatized, he, in some way as a man, may sometimes seem almost destined and programmed to pass the trauma on to others.

Though most victims of abuse do not themselves become abusers, a small minority do. In *Homecoming,* John Bradshaw writes, "Offender Behavior is the result of childhood violence and the suffering and unresolved grief of that abuse. The once powerless wounded child becomes the offender adult.... We have to understand that many forms of child abuse actually set up the child to be an offender. This is especially true of physical abuse, sexual abuse and severe emotional battering."[7]

Our clinical experience, supported by research, suggests that 97 percent of sexual perpetrators were sexually, physically, or severely emotionally abused as children or adolescents. The great majority of them, from 62 to 81 percent, were sexually abused.[8] When we do a perpetrator's psychosexual history and track how his abusive behavior developed, we almost always discover that the process began when he was first abused. His own abuse is not the only factor in this development, yet it is one of the key pieces of the puzzle of why someone becomes an abuser.

Although research results vary, it is estimated that approximately one in four women in the United States was sexually abused as a child or teen.[9] One in six men were sexually abused when young.[10] The perpetrators of this abuse are mostly male victims of abuse grown up to become abusers. This is a major part of the cycle of abuse that must be broken.

The priest in this story is one of these statistics. He was pulled into this cycle of abuse. His parents' emotional abandonment, his own sexual abuse, his mother's control and sexual shaming, the trauma of combat in World War II pulled him into this cycle. He vividly describes what it is like to be bedeviled by sexual addiction. He did not want to be sexual with himself, yet he felt compelled to be so. He was obsessed with both desiring to be sexual and wanting to fight it. He was so preoccupied with his internal struggle that his days felt "pointless" and "useless" until he gave into his compulsion. Having acted out sexually, he experienced a momentary good feeling and relief from his emotional pain and obsession. But fairly soon thereafter he felt great self-hatred and renewed emotional pain, which led to the next compulsion to medicate his pain with sex again.

Triggers Accelerate Addiction

All addictions and compulsive disorders are progressive. This means that over time more and more of the "drug," whatever that might be for the individual, is needed for the addict to experience the same high or level of self-medication. In sexual addiction, the addiction pushes the addict to seek more sex, the drug of the sex addict, by escalating to greater frequency or intensity of the sexual behavior. Sometimes an external trigger adds to this process. When this priest went away for graduate study, ironically in psychology, he was exposed to pornographic material. This escalated his sexual addiction to a new level of behavior, intensity, and shame. It flooded his already addicted mind with intense, graphic sexual images, some apparently child related. This new intensity and the increased shame linked with these images eventually built a compulsive desire to act out with children what he now imagined while compulsively masturbating.

Exposure to this material likely provoked a psychological process called "trauma repetition."[11] I see this frequently in my clients. Trauma repetition is characterized by an unconscious compulsion to do something over and over, even though it is destructive to self or others, that is rooted in or repeats the abuse that the person experienced as a child. Being exposed to material about people who abuse children triggered an unconscious reaction to this man's own abuse as a child. Since he had never dealt with or healed his wound, it would have triggered a process in which he would repeat and recreate in his adult mind and behavior the abuse trauma that he experienced as a child.

Tragically, this is what appears to have happened in the story of this man. Following the pornography trigger, his victimization, his sexual addiction, his internal anger at his mother — generalized to all women, his profound shame, and his social isolation fused into a dynamic of re-peating his own abuse in his sexual abuse of young girls. The unhealed child had become the father of the now abusive man.

A Pattern for Healing

While this man's story and the extent of the abuse he in-flicted is one of the worst I have heard from anyone I have treated in my twenty years of practicing psychotherapy, mercifully and paradoxically it is also one of the most hopeful and inspiring. With minimal professional help, this man gradually turned his life completely around. He stopped his abusive, offending behavior; eventually over-came his severe sexual addiction; restored his spirituality; devoted his life to simple service, prayer, and penance in reparation for his abusive behavior; and even became a catalyst for healing for some of his victims.

We see his recovery begin when he was imprisoned for the attempted rape of a disabled adult woman in the hos-pital where he was a chaplain, which he believes may have been an unconscious cry to be caught and stopped. The fear and shock of prison was an effective deterrent for his sexual abuse behavior. The sexual addiction, however, continued to torment him (and he continued to be at risk to reoffend and abuse children, although apparently he was able to control this behavior).

Relief and full recovery from his addiction finally came from two sources. First, his new bishop intervened at the request of one of his victims, and the priest voluntar-ily surrendered his faculties (or right) to function as a priest. This had a profound effect on him. He felt a huge weight lifted from him, apparently the shame and pressure to prove himself as a priest, which had been one of the core drivers of his addiction. He no longer had to please his mother. He was free to be an ordinary person. His compulsive masturbation finally ceased.

Soon afterward, he met a spiritual director who provided a program of practical and spiritual recovery from his addiction. He started to grow spiritually once again. He returned to prayer. He was finally able to stop the toxic sexual thoughts and images. He then began thirteen years of a very lonely yet positive life of service, prayer, and penance. During this time, at their initiative, he communicated with some of his now adult victims in hopes of helping them with their healing process. These communications were usually very painful for him, opening up old wounds and creating intense guilt about his past behavior. Yet he remained committed to meeting with the victims if they requested it. The meetings are one way he felt he made some amends for the abuse.

During the process of chronicling these stories, one of his victims requested a meeting with him. I was privileged to facilitate their meeting. It was profoundly moving. He apologized again (he had met with her once before). She accepted his apology and expressed her forgiveness and her concern for his well-being. He was able to answer some questions about the past that she felt would be helpful in her healing. I was able also to explain to her some aspects of his history and sickness that I felt would help in her healing. It was especially moving for her to hear for the first time that he too had been a victim of sexual abuse when he was a child. They parted with a palpable sense of peace and reconciliation in the room.

This kind of healing apology meeting between abuser and victim is, regrettably, rather rare. This one was a model for what could and should occur more often. The Church, I believe, should be fulfilling its gospel mission of healing and reconciliation by promoting more such healing interactions between priest abuser and victim. Our adversarial civil legal system cannot by its nature bring healing and closure. The Church with the help of appropriate professionals certainly could. Facilitated dialogue between victims and their abusers can help to heal the hurt and stop the ongoing circle of abuse.

Our hope is that this book itself can provide a real, if indirect, dialogue between victims and abusers. Our prayer has been that these stories will allow these priests to offer their apology for their abuse, to express their deep sorrow for what they have done, and to tell of their prayer for healing for their victims and the Church. We hope that victims, even though these priests may not be their particular abusers, may be able to hear their apology in a way that is healing for them.

In the stories of victims, perhaps they will hear some key that will further unlock their healing. These stories demonstrate that healing is possible for both the victims and the priest victim-abusers. They also show us that despite the tragedy of abuse, they do not have to be adversaries. They are fellow sufferers, both suffering in surprisingly similar ways, for very similar reasons, with a common path of healing.

Today this priest, now in his old age, has attained solid recovery and freedom from his addiction; he is free at last. He does have moments of intense guilt, remorse, and regret about his past abusive behavior, from which he will never be fully free. He is still suffering the consequences of his past sick, abusive behavior and of his own history as a victim of abuse and neglect. Yet a deepening peace is gathering within him. He continues to grow spiritually, living a simple life of service to fellow residents in his supervised recovery community. He prays daily for his victims, which is, as he says, "all that he knows to do" at this late stage of his life.

Four

A PRIEST
AND HIS WOUND

~~~~~~~

I have been different and a bit unusual right from the beginning. I was born nearly two months premature and weighed only three pounds. Back in the late thirties a baby that premature had a limited chance for survival. However, the hospital where I made my appearance had just purchased and installed an incubator. I was the first baby to use the new device, and it sustained my gift of life. But my mother was unable to nurse me, and the doctors had trouble developing a formula that I could keep down.

With a continual absence of food, I apparently cried a lot, and in my infant anger I stiffened and strained my abdomen and groin. At the age of six weeks I developed an abdominal hernia and had to undergo surgery. I was so tiny and the incision was so small the surgeon covered it with a Band-Aid. The hernia surgery was not successful, and I had to wear a truss for support until I was nearly six years old. The concern and emphasis on my genital area for the first six years of my life had an effect on me, and it was easy to focus on my penis during those early years.

I always saw myself as a victim even though I didn't know that word or understand its meaning when I was young.

Looking back, being victimized seems to be a part of how I lived many of the events of my life.

I feel the wounds of victimization in my past relations with my father. I never felt that he took a loving, caring interest in me. I was the first child, and because I was so small and so sickly, he did not know how to connect with me. My mother, her sister, and her mother doted on me and tried to meet my needs. Perhaps my dad felt that with all the women fussing over me, he could not get close to me. Also, I am sure he had feelings of incompetence as a father. I was such a tiny child and then the next child, a son, born two years later, lived only two days. Another boy was born when I was four. I always believed my dad was closer to him, though he too was sickly.

As a young child I developed a type of workaholism to compensate for the seeming lack of attention and love I received from my father. I did many things in the family to prove that I was capable and lovable. That didn't work like I wished, but as with any addiction, it did not stop me from overworking, especially when I wanted and needed to be accepted and loved.

The summer before I was six, I was playing with some friends and we lifted a heavy pole, and I ruptured the other side of my groin area. I was rushed to the hospital and surgeons did a double surgery repairing both hernias. Although there was a lot of pain in the groin area after surgery, the constant treatment, touching, and attention reinforced the childhood attention to that specific area and I enjoyed the mix of pain-pleasure that went with it.

DEVELOPING FRIENDSHIPS

Sometime after that second hernia surgery, while playing with my best friend, he convinced me to allow him to touch me in the genital and anal areas. I was afraid that my folks would know, but I also enjoyed it. From this experience I came to believe that when you really care about someone, this kind of activity is all right, even required. This friend taught me how to masturbate by rubbing my penis against some hard surface. For years after that, masturbation in this fashion was the way I went to sleep nightly by rubbing against the mattress. Once my father caught me doing it and commanded that I never do it again. My childlike mind reasoned, "He won't give me time, love, and attention, and when I find something I like, he wants to take it away." Once again, the victim. Always the victim!

During the years I was thirteen and fourteen, a different best friend and I did many things together. Because he was my best friend and because of my old belief, the closer we got the more inclined we were to play genital games. I believed that's what good friends who cared about one another did. My friend and I developed a game that was somewhat sadomasichistic, though we never did anything to hurt one another. One day, I asked my friend to do something sexual to me that he was not comfortable with. He did, but we never played the game again after that. He was becoming interested in a particular girl and a priest told me in confession that if I wanted to go to the seminary I had to cease such practices. Because I felt called to priesthood, I did cease all of these games and even the masturbation that I had done for years.

77

During my high school years, I never saw myself as gay. I didn't know the sexual meaning of the word and didn't know what gay people did or that there were such people. But I do remember the attraction I felt for other guys in my class and in my school. Though I seldom had sexual thoughts about them, sometimes that sexual attraction surfaced. I remember covering the basketball games for the local paper and enjoying being in the locker room, especially after the games when the guys were taking showers.

I had no sexual interest in girls. I had many good friends who were girls, but was not drawn to them in a sexual way. I was not involved in playing sports, but was interested and involved in theater. I don't believe I was effeminate, and I don't think others saw me as that. I was a class leader and officer. I finished high school with high honors and awards of distinction. Though almost no one knew of my plans, I was now ready to enter the diocesan seminary.

What drew me to the priesthood? I had been an altar boy in my youth. I respected priests and was influenced by them. I worked around the church helping out and cleaning. That was what a good Catholic boy did, and even with my masturbation and sexual games, I saw myself as a "good Catholic boy." After high school I applied to the diocese. They required that you come to the seminary the last Saturday in June for a full day of testing and interviews. I passed all the tests except a fifteen-minute physical where the doctor determined I had a heart murmur. So I was rejected.

When I learned of my rejection, I immediately entered the hospital where my local physician put me through numerous tests checking my heart. He found no murmur, but I was quite thin and he said that because of this, there was an echo in the stethoscope. Once again, I was a victim.

This time the Church victimized me. I went through some deep spiritual pain since I saw it as not only the Church but also God rejecting me and my desire for the priesthood. But whenever I have been told I can't do something, there is a part of me that says, "Oh no? Watch!"

By Easter I determined that I was going to try for priesthood again. If the diocese didn't want me, perhaps I was being called to a religious priesthood. I applied to a religious community. Also, though I did not understand it then, I wanted love from a man. Because of this, I was drawn to an organization dedicated to Jesus. The emphasis on Jesus' love for everyone certainly reflected my yearning for male acceptance and love. I don't think that this was clear to me at the time, but it seems that such feelings and influences were a hidden part of my choice. The vocation people from this group seemed to take a special interest in me. I left my newspaper job and entered the seminary of this religious community.

My mother was happy that I wanted to enter a seminary. She was a lifelong Catholic, and the tradition of the first boy being given to the service of God was a part of that Catholic tradition. My father, who converted to Catholicism when he married my mother, did not feel the same. He did everything he could to convince me to stay home after my summer vacation. He purchased me a car to entice me to give up ideas of priesthood and stay home. Once again, when someone tried to stop me, that only made my desires and efforts to continue stronger.

I was not involved in any genital activity during my years of seminary. I had made a vow of celibacy, and I tried to keep it. I masturbated several times, but even that was not a regular practice. I was attracted to several of my fellow seminarians, and I developed a close friendship with them, but there was never any genital activity.

One fellow seminarian was five years younger than I was. We seemed to be drawn to one another. We spent time talking and sharing in the privacy of my room. I remember hugging him and once or twice kissing him, but we were clothed in our religious habits and nothing else ever happened. Such activities excited me to erections and sometimes, later at night, brought on masturbation. I wanted to sexually touch him, yet did not want to lose his friendship. We never did anything genital, and, though he seemed to be gay, I never knew whether it was true. We were all men gathered in a closed and exclusive lifestyle. When you were lonely and in need of friendship and affection, you had no one in the seminary of my day to turn to except to another man.

"ADOPTING" SONS

During my theology studies I was involved in teaching catechetics to children. I was attracted to some of the male junior high students, and I made friends with them. Nothing sexual ever happened, but, ominously, I was learning how to appeal to and entice these boys and have them attach to me as friends.

I was ordained a priest when I was twenty-eight years old. My first assignment was in parish ministry. I was placed in charge of youth ministry and was connected with the grade school, in daily contact with youth as a teacher and a bus driver as well as the priest who celebrated Mass for them on a regular basis. I made friends with young boys and their families. I thought that I was doing what I should do as a priest, but, in looking back, I see that in some cases I was setting them up.

One boy was ten years old, blond, blue-eyed, and looking for a man's attention and affection. I don't believe his father had much contact with and concern for him. I remembered how that felt, and I did not want that to happen to this beautiful, loving boy. I befriended him and spent a great deal of time with him. There were others also that I became close to. One other family, who had five boys from about six years to eighteen, became a close part of my life. During this time, their father died of cancer. I was especially close to the nine-year-old and the twelve-year-old. I took them to various activities, to my home to visit my parents, and even on vacation to the seashore. My family welcomed them and cared for them as if they were my children. When I was with my family on vacation, my father complained that I slept with one of the boys when I could have used a single bed and let them share the double. I resisted his suggestion since I wanted the twelve-year-old to be close to me and even wanted to give him back, chest, and belly rubs. No genital contact ever happened. But in my imagination, the genital touching was done and was enjoyed. This young man did not see anything wrong with our relationship and, at that point, I don't think I did either.

After a year in parish ministry, I was reassigned to vocation work. I covered twenty states in the eastern United States. I spent untold hours with young men and boys. I brought them from the East Coast to the Midwest to spend a weekend in the high school seminary. I became very close to many of them, but nothing sexual ever happened between us. I can see now that, as long as I had young men and boys around me, I did not act out with any of them;

just their presence seemed to be enough. However, in the privacy of my own room and comfort of my own bed I did masturbate to the fantasy of the relationships I wanted with the boys.

After four years in vocation work, I was transferred to what had been a seminary, which we were changing into a retreat house and conference center. I again worked much too hard. Though I did some programs for youth, I did not have young people around me all the time as I had in previous assignments. A few weeks after I was in this new assignment, I met a family after Mass. The second son of the family, about twelve years old, was the most beautiful young man I had ever seen. With his blond hair and blue eyes he was similar to my young friend whom I had left back in the parish. I had a long, happy, and loving relationship with the boy and his whole family, which included another brother and two sisters. I spent over eight years at this assignment and I helped the boy to learn to read since he had a learning disability. I did many things with the two boys; swimming, fishing, and camping were just a few. I never did anything sexual with them, but I fantasized about the possibility.

During the time I was director of the conference center, one of the adult members of my religious community was stationed with me. I fell in love with him. He had the blond hair and blue eyes that always attracted me and had a very pleasant personality. He and I developed a lasting friendship and did many activities together. When we went on vacations together, we often slept in the same double bed. We engaged in mutual massage of backs and fronts but did not approach the genital area. One night after I had returned from a trip, he picked me up from the airport. We were visiting at the home of one of my relatives. After we had

82

gone to bed, I leaned over and kissed him and he kissed me back. The next night, even though I thought he was asleep, I reached over to rub his chest and stomach. Gradually my hand slipped down to his genital area, and I began to rub him there. He signaled to me to continue. This began a sexual relationship involving contact several different times in the next few years. He eventually left the community. I was transferred to another location, and our contact became infrequent. However, I feel we are still close, even though his life has gone in a different direction from mine.

When I was next transferred, I became involved in a new diocese and within six months headed the adult educational department. I was also superior of the local religious community and held numerous offices for the local bishop. My workaholism surfaces when I want to be liked and be special. This has happened since I was a boy, and it certainly happened in this ministry.

As a result, I was very busy and much in need of someone to have time and fun with. I did not go looking for another priest, but I was attracted to one of the young boys who regularly served for me at the parish Mass. This boy came from a broken family and needed the influence of a caring male. We went from Mass together, to lawn and garden care, to fishing together, to food shopping, and house cleaning, any activity that we could do together. He, like others who preceded him, became my adopted son. I loved him. Some professionals have scoffed at my assertion that I called my relationship with this young man love, but I did and do love him. I did not mean to hurt him, but rather meant to give him some sexual instructions. That was my rationalization. This, unfortunately, developed into sexual activity.

The friendship and sexual activity continued, off and on, for about five years.

When his younger brother was about fourteen years old, he told me that he "wanted a relationship with me like his brother had." He didn't know what he was asking for, but as things developed he too did all sorts of things with me including sexual activities. There was a sense of caring and support along with the sexual touching. He worked for me at the house and in the offices of the diocese where I was director. Later he served as a youth minister. He also served as a church repairman and as a constant friend. These two brothers were sometimes my sexual victims, helped with all sorts of work and ministry efforts, and served as "adopted" sons. As they grew up and grew away from me, my continued need and watching eye saw other boys and young men who could replace these older ones.

NEVER REALLY FREE

I went back into full-time parish ministry in a small downtown parish where transients and poor people were all around us. Drug users and dealers, youth gangs, and gay men also frequented the area. I spent about half my time trying to find food for individuals and families. I became close to one young man from a family of four boys and another boy from a family of three. We spent time working together, and they often stayed overnight at the parish house. When that happened, they shared a bed with me, and we engaged in mutual massage. I tried to French-kiss one boy, and he rejected my efforts. I touched the other one in the genital area on several occasions. They revealed these events to a youth minister and to their parents, and I was arrested. This was the beginning of over ten years in and out of prison, mental hospitals, restricted communities, and limited freedoms. I finally had to face my sexuality, my addictions, and my abuse activities.

During my years of ministry, I had served as a part-time chaplain at a prison and at a mental health facility. I thought I knew what such facilities were like, but really I had no idea till I became an inmate. Prison life was dangerous, so I was urged to keep my history, and my priesthood, secret. Some of the officers tried to help me remain unknown. Other officers were cruel and didn't seem to care whether I was unknown or not. Prison was filled with loneliness. There is very little trust in such a facility even among fellow inmates. You may develop some friendships, but very few and very carefully.

I did reveal that I was a teacher and was able to teach men who were working toward getting their GED. I also was able to help men who were unable to read. I felt useful being able to help these men. When the newspapers told my story, my life was in danger in the state facility where I was located. The authorities had to move me immediately and lock me down in another facility.

After I had served my time, I was freed from the physical bars of prison, but there are many kinds of incarcerations and imprisonments from which I will never be free. I did not see the boys and young men with whom I had sexual activities as sex objects but rather as people whom I cared about and loved. I still care about them. I don't want to have sex with them any longer, and I am sorry for the hurt I caused them. I would like to erase those hurtful events, but I never want to erase the rest of the relationships I had with those men, the part that was good and caring. I pray for them and their families. There is nothing else I know to do to help heal the pain I have caused my victims.

Because of my actions and the media coverage, I have lost contact, respect, and love from many people whom I ministered to and cared about. Even members of my family will have no contact with me. I admit that what I did was wrong, illegal, and immoral. But the way the media covered these events was often full of half-truths. My own sexual activities, the media, and the civil suits that have been brought against me closed the doors on my friendships and relationships.

My Church, which Christ challenged to forgive "seventy times seven," has turned their backs on me and other men who have been accused of sexual activities with youth. The bishops seem to be so afraid of losing money in civil suits and lowered collections that they are sometimes very unforgiving of the sins of their clergy. At all ordinations men becoming priests hear, "You are a priest forever." But many dioceses have done their best to laicize any offenders and dismiss them from the only adult life and experience they have ever known. Forced out on their own, ex-priests are more likely to offend again since there is little support and acceptance of them. There is also little psychological help given to these men who are forced to leave the priesthood. The bishops want them out of sight and out of mind. There are very few places for ex-priests to live, since many states have some version of Megan's Law, and neighbors revolt at having these men in their area. There are few facilities that will take in such men.

I have often thought that it is good that St. Peter was not a member of the American clergy. He denied Jesus three times. I am sure that the current bishops would never allow him to be pope, and the righteous people would not want his leadership. He would probably be laicized and sent to some other area with hopes that the neighbors would accept him. A church founded by a God-man who was forgiving and accepting, especially of sexual sins, seems to have been forgotten.

I learned in prison to live one day at a time. Sometimes to survive, it was living one hour at a time. Today, I am a resident in one of the few facilities that are for priests and religious who have been charged with or found guilty of sexual abuse of youth. I live with other men who have similar histories. As I am sometimes, some of them are filled with much anger, bitterness, and frustration at their loss of freedom. Others are accepting, caring, forgiving, prayerful, and almost saintly. Their past sinful experiences affect each man differently.

I am lonely sometimes. I would like more freedom since I believe I served punishment time in prison. By and large, I try to live one day at a time, and I try to gift others with my talents and abilities. I have had anger with the media, the state, the Church, and even God, but each of these angers has been and is being worked out. I have had many capable counselors to help me with these issues.

I have learned to accept my homosexuality. I see it not as something I have chosen, but as a gift from God. If that is like the many other God-given gifts I have received, I need to rejoice in it and use it for my good and the good of others. Though my sexual orientation certainly was involved in the sexual activities of which I am guilty, I do not believe that gay men are more likely to be a danger to children or youth. I did not abuse because I am gay. I abused because I was sick. I hope that homosexuality will be researched further and become better understood.

Let me close by again saying I am sorry for harming the youth I abused and for hurting any other people who were offended by my actions. I hope that forgiveness will happen across our world and a prayerful peace will come upon us all.

Ψ COMMENTARY

I am sure that many readers instinctively feel revulsion at this priest's statement that he loved and cared for his victims and saw them as adopted sons. His being sexual with them was certainly not a loving act. In being sexual with his young male victims, he used them for his own emotional, sexual, addictive needs, in denial of the harm that he was causing them. This man can now see this and admits it in his story. At the same time, it is possible that he did care for and love them, although there was much distortion and personal need in this love.

It is a myth, which most people hold, that all sexual abuse comes from cruelty and total disregard for the child. In some cases, as in this story, the abuse comes from crossing sexual boundaries in the midst of a close, otherwise caring relationship.

It is another common myth that most sex abusers of children or adolescents are strangers to the child, seeking out their victims in public places or private homes. A small minority of abusers fit this profile. We see this type of sex offender in the horrific headline stories of children being abducted, sexually exploited, and sometimes killed. In our clinical experience most abuse is perpetrated by some-one the child knows, trusts, and has a relationship with:

fathers, uncles, cousins, siblings, youth workers, teachers, ministers, priests. Almost all the clerical perpetrators that we have treated, or whose victims we have treated, are relational abusers, someone the child or adolescent has a relationship with and has come to trust. A few of the high-profile cases have involved priests who had over a hundred victims each. This is especially abhorrent, and it is not relational abuse. These are classic, fixated, exclusive pedophiles. However, most priest abusers have far fewer victims (one to eight is the most common range).[12] The abuse is done in the context of a trusting relationship, which can, in fact, be more emotionally damaging than stranger abuse, although less physically violent.

Sadly, what this priest describes in his story of caring relationships turned abusive is all too common. Even if there is love in a relationship, if there is abuse, there is great harm to the child. In some ways there is more harm done. It creates profound confusion and shame when the child feels both sexually used and loved in the relationship. One of the most damaging aspects of sexual abuse of a child is the betrayal of trust. This is even more severe when the child has felt loved and cared for by his or her abuser.

The priest in this story says he saw his victims not as sex objects, but as young people he cared about and loved. In fact, he did see them and use them as sex objects even as he acted caringly toward them. How can this happen? How can anyone — a father, clergyman, youth worker, or any trusted adult — be truly caring or loving toward a child and eventually become so abusive? This man's story provides a classic picture of the answer.

We first see the origins of the sexual obsession in this priest's very early medical problems. The hernia soon after his birth and the subsequent injuries and medical treatment inadvertently constituted a form of trauma that over-focused the young child on his genitals and on genital pleasure. Concern about his medical problems may have created an early obsessional connection in his childhood mind between sexual sensation and being cared about. We see this already fully developed around six years of age when he engages in sex play and exploration, a fairly common occurrence with children, with his best friend. The young child already believes "that when you really care about someone this kind of activity is all right, even required." In his mind, this is what good friends do with each other. This becomes a key thought distortion for the rationalization of later abusive behavior.

Early on, sexual sensation and self-stimulation became a way to compensate for and soothe his emotional pain, especially his father's rejection. Later, he mentors and "adopts" young boys, especially those who, like him, were not fathered. In a sense he is also emotionally wounded by the "doting" he received from his mother, aunt, and grandmother. The combination of his father's rejection and these women's doting leaves the young boy with a strong need throughout his life to be wanted and to be special to someone. This is linked with a self-perception, most likely from his early medical problems and his father's rejection, as being a victim. All of these emotional issues became fused with his early sexual experiences so that being sexual becomes the way to feel good, wanted, and special and in control.

Although he does not refer to it much, the difficulty of growing up gay in a culture that did not even acknowledge the existence of homosexuality and certainly shamed and rejected it would have added to his psychosexual difficulties. The need to hide a sexual secret about which one feels shame intensifies that secret's power and also blocks the normal learning about how to maturely handle the attendant sexual feelings and attractions.

He again engaged in sexual exploration with a friend when they were teenagers. This reinforced the connection in his mind between being close and being sexual with a friend. He suppressed this belief, his psychosexual development, his woundedness, and his need for relationship when he pursued becoming a priest and entering the seminary. This is what happened too often in the past in religious formation in Catholic seminaries. The candidate, heterosexual or homosexual, was simply expected to put aside and ignore his human needs, especially sexual and relational, in the service of his call. What is otherwise a wonderfully incarnational and earthy religion has sometimes expected its clerical leadership to be anti-incarnational and superhuman. During seminary years, these issues did reemerge for the author to some degree in an attraction to a classmate and in attractions to male junior high students that he met in the course of teaching catechetics. Nothing happened genitally; however, there was some level of fantasizing and sexual arousal and masturbation to these fantasies.

After ordination, the attraction to young boys grew. At first, he simply made friends with boys and their families as a part of his ministry. However, his obsession grew, and he developed a pattern of grooming potential victims and violating healthy boundaries. At first, there was no genital touching. However, he became overly close and attracted to a young boy whose father was neglectful, a characteristic of all of his victims and, of course, of himself. He crossed physical privacy boundaries by giving the boy massages and sharing a bed with him. Nothing genital happened with this boy except in the man's imagination. What is allowed repeatedly in fantasy often finds a way to be acted out in behavior.

The close but nongenital relationships with young men and boys continued. The fantasy and the self-stimulation continued as well. Genuine caring ministry to these youngsters was occurring; indeed, in general this author seemed to be otherwise a very caring, gifted, and effective priest who provided great help to the young. Yet his sickness festered. The next progression in his illness happened in the context of a friendship with an adult, a member of his religious community. The relationship became a mutually consensual genital relationship. Crossing this boundary made it easier to later cross sexual boundaries with young people.

Pedophiles

A note here about pedophilia. Many people have the misconception that adults who sexually abuse children have no other sexual interest. This is true of some pedophiles who are fixated only on children. Many people who abuse children, however, do have sexual and emotional relationships with adults. Generally, we have not used the term "pedophile" in referring to the priests in these stories. It is a term that is widely misused in regard to priests who abuse. To clarify, pedophiles are sexually attracted to children thirteen or under of either one gender or both. Only about 10 percent of pedophiles are fixated, or exclusive, pedophiles.[13] That is, they are sexually attracted to children only. This is the classic picture most people have of the pedophile. This type of pedophile is especially sick, is fixated on a certain age and type of child, and tends to have a large number of victims.

According to Thomas G. Plante and Gerald McGlone about 90 percent of individuals who have abused children are actually nonexclusive pedophiles.[14] They have acted out sexually with children and are also sexually active with adults. They are often sexually compulsive or addicted individuals who are not primarily attracted to children as sex objects, but whose sexual behavior has gotten so out of control that they violate children's privacy boundaries and sexually abuse them. These adults usually have a smaller number of victims than fixated or exclusive pedophiles. The term "ephebophile" is used to refer to individuals who are attracted to adolescents, ages fourteen to eighteen, again of either sex or both sexes.[15] Ephebophiles generally have fewer victims and are less sexually fixated on the age group than exclusive pedophiles.

Priests Who Abuse

What are the facts about priests who abuse? Studies have shown that priest perpetrators of abuse are more likely to be ephebophiles, that is, they have sexually abused adolescents, than pedophiles. The estimates suggest between 57 percent and 80 percent of priests who are sexually abusive are ephebophiles and 20–44 percent are pedophiles.[16] Regarding gender of the victims, it is variously estimated that 80 percent of priest abusers molest males and 20 percent molest females, or that 68 percent molest males, 20 percent molest females, and 12 percent abuse both.[17] In our own therapy practice, working with survivors of clerical abuse, there has been a considerably higher percentage of female victims than these studies report. To complete the statistical picture of priest abusers in relation to sexual orientation, one study found that 44 percent were homosexual, 40 percent were heterosexual, 15 percent were bisexual, 2 percent were asexual.[18]

Much of the research into the priest sexual abuse situation is not yet definitive, and the results vary widely in some categories. However, we know enough to state categorically that most of the myths that the media has suggested and that stick in many people's minds are wrong and not based on the facts. For example, many people assume that a large percentage of Roman Catholic priests have abused children. Various studies estimate that between 1.8 percent to 6 percent of the 47,000 American Catholic priests have sexually abused minors.[19] This would mean that approximately one to three thousand priests in the United States have abused (this study did not have any statistics about the incidence of abuse by Catholic religious brothers or religious sisters, groups not yet as fully studied in regard to this problem). This is, of course, too many and a serious problem. Nevertheless, male clergy of Protestant, Jewish, or Muslim faiths who have sexually abused minors are found at about the same percentage. The statistics are the same for men who work as Boy Scout leaders, coaches, or other youth workers.[20] A Catholic priest is no more likely than any other male entrusted with children to abuse them, despite the impression currently held by many people.

At the End of the Cycle

The final chapter in the development of this author's full-blown sexual addiction and obsession with children unfolded when he again was ministering to an emotionally needy, father-starved young boy. Another period of his workaholism made him more vulnerable to his sexual addiction. He crossed the final boundary and became genitally sexual with the boy under the rationalization of giving him sexual instruction. Once this boundary was violated, it became easier to cross it again and an ongoing pattern of abuse became compulsive, recurring with different young boys with whom he developed overly close relationships.

All the elements of an addictive, sexually offensive sickness were now in place. The process that began with a young boy feeling deeply hurt and affected by the trauma of early genitally focused medical problems and his father's rejection had produced an adult man, a priest father figure, who hurt other young boys. The cycle of abuse came full circle again. He was now fully out of control and did not stop until he was caught and arrested. As with alcoholics, who often stop only when they hit bottom, compulsive abusers, even priests, are so in the grip of their addiction that they frequently cannot stop on their own.

Tragically, of course, the direst consequence was to the young victims. I believe that this priest truly cared for his

95

victims, did help them in many ways, and truly did not mean them harm. It was the measure of his addictive, distorted thinking that he did not see the grave harm he did inflict on them. It is a measure of his recovery that he does now see and acknowledge the harm he caused the young men. He sees the destructive power of his addiction and works hard to stay in recovery in the restricted environment that he lives in. His rationalization, denial, and compulsive behaviors are now largely gone. What remains is living with what he has done to his victims and with what he has lost. Today, he lives a rather simple life focused on healthy, adult friendship and acts of service within his recovery community.

Five

A PRIEST
OUTSIDE THE CIRCLE

I am very proud of the fact that I was born six months after my parents were married. It gave me the feeling that I had a lot to do with getting my mom's parents to approve of my folks' marriage. One of the great joys of my almost forty years of active priestly ministry has been my ability to bring people together, not only at Eucharist, but in any other way I could.

I was not only my parents' first child but also the first grandchild and the first nephew. Needless to say, I got a lot of attention and was cheered on by the whole family in every new step I took growing up. We weren't wealthy, but we pretty much had all we needed and some beyond because my dad always had a good blue-collar job. He worked very hard outside the house and he also spent plenty of great time with me and my three brothers and one sister as they came along every five years or so.

We expressed our love very openly. Dad would never leave for work or come home from work without a kiss and hug for Mom and me. I was reasonably punished when I did something that called for it; my greatest punishment was not getting Mom's good-night kiss. I would lie in bed crying until she broke down and gave me the kiss so I could sleep.

I loved to curl up in Dad's lap and have him read me stories, the comics, and, later, books. Dad and I would wrestle and box, with heavily padded gloves. Mom, Dad, and I took long walks on Sunday afternoons, sometimes to sit, along with aunts, uncles, and cousins, on my grandparents' front steps. These were always great times and laid the foundation for what, later on, would influence my model of Church: people joined together with each other in love, joy, and sharing.

The question at our house on Sunday morning was never, "Are we going to Mass today?" but, "What Mass are we going to?" Dad was active in the Holy Name Society. He and I printed their one-sheet newsletter in the rectory basement. I was enthralled being in the rectory. On Sunday mornings, after the Masses, Dad and I handed the parish newsletters out to people.

DEGREES OF ATTRACTION

In my Catholic grade school, we started every day with Mass. It was a delight to have one of the priests come into our classroom once a week to teach the religion classes. I especially looked forward to our newly ordained associate pastor coming in. He could draw well, and after school he would hang out on the corner with a couple dozen of us, playing with us, doing magic tricks, and telling us stories. His car hardly ever left his garage without being filled with kids. I knew as far back as I can remember that I wanted to be a priest like him.

I played with friends, but, because of poor eyesight, I was never any good at sports. I was always the last person chosen for a team in our sandlot games. I was usually given a position in which I could do the least damage. From then to the present, I have always felt on the fringe of my peers, outside the circle. I compensated by finding other ways to spend my time: playing with my Dad and our model train set, working as a librarian throughout seminary, and preaching and writing as a priest. The Lord may well have used my fringe status as one of the factors that drew me to the priesthood.

Before I ever heard of the word "homosexual," I knew I was strongly attracted to other boys, and later, to men. I never felt bad about that. As I came to recognize later, God blesses each person with a mixture of masculine and feminine qualities and degrees of attraction to those of the opposite or same sex. I feel sexual orientation is no different than hair color. I never made an issue of my sexual attraction to other boys as a kid, never acted out on these attractions, didn't talk to anybody about it, and didn't feel a victim of society or the Church, then or now. I am grateful that God has given me a good number of what some might consider "feminine" qualities: compassion, sympathy, concern for the needy and their lack of power, position, or possessions.

In the high school boarding seminary I went to, I felt we had some very weird rules about modesty. When we wanted to change our clothes, we couldn't do it in the dormitory, but had to go to one of the bathroom stalls. Going to bed, we changed into our nightclothes in bed, under our sheets. The showers were all individual, with an attached cubicle in which to get dressed. We played flag football and had a "no touch" rule. This just built up my interest in fellow seminarians to whom I was attracted. This suppression heightened my desire and fantasies of seeing and being with kids in the nude. As I grew into adulthood, my sexual interest remained stunted at this level.

THE GIFT OF FAMILIES

I have always wanted to be a priest. As a priest, I have always regarded myself as a servant, coach, or bandleader of the Lord's priestly people. I have an inborn drive to change things and to help people and improve situations. I put all I had into leading the community at liturgy to appreciate God's love and many blessings, to celebrate the liturgies with life, enthusiasm, and vitality. I enjoy leading God's people in celebrating the Eucharist, and especially feeding my brothers and sisters with the life-changing Word of God.

That's one of the reasons I asked my superiors to assign me to the ministry of preaching parish missions and appeals for our foreign missions for sixteen years. At week-long missions I had the opportunity to preach to virtually the same congregation for four hours. The basic theme was that you are gifted, and you are called to use these gifts with the support and in support of the gifts of your family and Church to continue God's saving work in the world. I tied these same themes together in each Sunday homily.

Because of my deep relationships with families throughout my priesthood, perhaps rooted in my prenatal experience of bringing my parents closer together, I have never felt lonely in priesthood. Some priests say their lives are lonely. I've rarely experienced that or allowed myself to experience it. My greatest pain in the priesthood came when a thousand people or more would pass me by on the way out of church, after I had just fed them with the Word of God, the Body and Blood of Christ, and as much of myself as I could put into it, and nobody asked, "Father, could you join us for dinner today?" I couldn't bear being in the rectory by myself on a Friday, Saturday, or Sunday night. I knew it was then that the Lord's families were together, and I as "Father" wanted to be with them. If I didn't have an invitation, I would get on the phone and call people until I found someone who would be "family" to me that day. I served as team priest in Cursillo, Marriage Encounter, Engaged Encounter, Youth Encounters, Parish Renewal Weekends, and the Charismatic Renewal. I considered each to be another gift of God to his people and me. And I became part of some great families through these experiences. But therein was my downfall.

There were certain families with kids that I visited often, dropping in for dinner and spending the evening. I loved to rough-house with the kids, the way I used to rough-house with my dad when I was a kid. Eventually, I came to feel like a brother to the parents and an uncle to the kids in these families.

Several times, we drank, not enough to inebriate me, but enough to lower my inhibitions. Sometimes I was asked to stay over in the same room as their boy or they would let me take him home with me for a sleep-over. I usually started by giving the boy a back rub or having a tickling contest with him. This often ended up in fondling him inappropriately. Sometimes I took several boys out with me for a weeklong camping trip, so much did the parents trust me. In our tent or cabin I often abused them in the same way or waited until I thought they were asleep and then fondled them. For the rest of my life, I will regret the abuse of those kids, the resultant psychological and social harm I did them, and the betrayal of their and their parents' trust. I hurt them more than if I had stolen all they had.

LOVE GONE AWRY

I wanted this to stop but felt unable to stop it, being in ministry in one location and in such close relationship with families. So I asked to be assigned to a preaching ministry in which I would be on the move every week and not be able to enter into relationships with families. This left me traveling, usually in my car by myself. It helped greatly to reduce the abuse, though occasionally an opportunity offered itself and my addiction kicked in again.

I thought I had a real love for these kids, but now I realize I was manipulating them and their families for my own gratification. My love had gone awry. I was inappropriately satisfying my desire for physical touch and closeness. I was also, I see now, trying to compensate for my experience as a kid of being out of the circle of my peers. It was a most inappropriate rage that burned within me about my past rejection. There may have even been an element of vengeance in my actions for being left out and rejected by my childhood peers. It was a very destructive way of attaining my childhood and adolescent desire to be accepted in the circle and be close to other kids.

During the years that my sexual addiction was active, I felt a split in my life. God was pretty fully in my life, but I was letting my addiction keep him out of a very important corner of it. I was very much aware of that corner, but I let the addiction build almost insurmountable walls around it. I felt, and believe I was, like an alcoholic, powerless to let God break into that corner. I believed in, experienced, and preached about a God of infinite and unconditional love. I felt a deep and personal intimacy with the God in whom I lived, and moved, and had my being. God was not distant, but as close a part of me and the world and people around me as the air we breathe. In prayer I constantly expressed my love for God. Yet I knew what I was doing was contrary to God's will. I compartmentalized this facet of my life. When I went to confession, I merely confessed touching another inappropriately. I didn't go to confession often, and when I did, it was to a different priest who didn't know me. I didn't have a spiritual director with whom I would be honest and who would challenge me to stop my behavior. When I did go to confession, I sincerely did want to stop and asked the Lord to help me. Through the grace of God, I was able to stop the abuse on my own. However, I knew I was still sick and needed professional help and might abuse again without it. Yet I could not make myself seek that help. Eventually, God further answered my prayers and got me this help through the intervention of some of those I abused and their parents.

I had minimized the seriousness of the abuse, thinking all I was doing was teaching these kids. They never told me they didn't like it or told me to stop. This kind of activity with a particular teen usually stopped when they got old enough to get a job, car, or girlfriend, and our contact diminished.

Now, after years of treatment and much reading, I have come to realize and deeply regret the tremendous harm I did to those kids, the harm it caused them in distancing themselves from their parents by not telling their parents of my activity, the harm it caused them in not being able to trust those they should be able to trust, the harm in their developing and maintaining stable, personal relationships. My actions may have caused some of them to abuse alcohol and drugs. Some of them never got married; others did and got divorced. I would be surprised if any of them were still going to church. I can hardly imagine the anger that must rise in them when they simply see a priest.

I only had the opportunity to meet one of my victims, who was in therapy at the same time I was. As part of his therapy, he was asked to confront his abuser. He phoned me one day and did so. I asked if he thought it would help his recovery if we both met together with one of our therapists. He said it might. Eventually, we met with my therapist. We were both very emotional. I told him of my sorrow for what I had done to him. I knew there was no way to adequately express this sorrow. He did not express anger during our session, but I imagine he has plenty of it. I hope he felt better after our meeting. I know I did.

Thank God, there were many families with whom I had relationships that were totally wholesome. The difference becomes most hurtful when I am going through my address book writing out my Christmas cards. Some names bring very happy memories and others deep sorrow. I can't send cards to those whom I have hurt. I bind these individuals and families together only in my prayer. I know many of their hearts feel the pain that past contact with me still causes them.

This loss of valuable relationships extends even into my immediate family. My mother was deeply hurt and disappointed when she discovered what I had done. On my first visit home after I had been in therapy for almost a year and a half I was very nervous and frightened. I felt like the prodigal son, not the youngest, but the oldest, and a priest, coming home after I had badly hurt many people and lost my ability to ever again publicly minister as a priest. We were both weeping as our eyes met each other's. I couldn't say a word until Mom tearfully said, "I know what you've done and know how wrong it was, but you are my son and I'll never stop loving you." I felt a great relief that she knew, deep grief for the sorrow I had caused her, and a tremendous appreciation for the God-like love and forgiveness she was showing me. I loved her and my father deeply throughout my life, but this experience of her love deepened my love beyond telling.

But this sadly was not the experience with all of my family. I have three brothers and a sister. One brother has remained on good terms with me. My sister and other two brothers stopped all contact. By God's grace, the brother to whom I am closest has begun to open up again. But communication is completely closed between me and my sister and other brothers. I pray that God's healing power eventually works in all of us, especially so my Mom might see her family together again. I don't blame my siblings for this breakdown of our relationships; I take total responsibility for it. It was my abusive actions that brought about this breakdown. This lack of harmony with my own family helps me to identify the distance I caused my victims to feel with their families.

I would meet with any of my victims, if it might help in their healing. My victims are hardly ever out of my mind, even after twenty years or more. I have been in a recovery program for the last five years, which keeps them always on my mind and I'm glad of that. I don't ever want to forget those I hurt. Now I have a prayerful concern for them which is true and healthy.

CONFESSION AND PRAYER

The abuse went on for over ten years with a number of boys. I was always fearful that one of them would tell their parents or another adult, which would end my priestly ministry, severely hurt my family, and put me in serious trouble with the law, probably ending in my incarceration. Fortunately for me, but unfortunately for the boys I continued to abuse, none of them ever spoke up, though I never asked or threatened them to keep quiet.

It was about ten years after my period of abusing ended that one of them told his parents, and they told another set of parents. The fathers of the two boys asked me to get together for lunch one day and, before going into the restaurant, asked me if this was true. They were expecting me to deny it, but I tearfully admitted that it was true. I expressed my sorrow, for all that could do. They were not interested in going to the police, just wanting to be assured that this was still not going on. I assured them that it had stopped, by God's grace, some ten years earlier. They suggested that I enter into counseling with a psychologist they knew. I did see him on an outpatient basis, periodically, for a couple years.

During all this time, no word of my deviant behavior made it to my religious superiors. Finally, another ten years later, four of the boys, now men, and two sets of their parents made allegations to my provincial. He gave me copies of the allegations and removed me from active ministry, as he had to do. This hurt a lot, because I so loved my preaching ministry. But I see that it was a very minimal hurt compared to the immense hurt I had caused my victims.

I was immediately sent for psychological evaluation and then treatment in a monitored living situation, where I have been for five years now. Being here has allowed the Lord to work in me in marvelous ways. I first saw the place as a prison. Then the Lord helped me to see it as a monastery in which I could continue ministry, the ministry of prayer. The residents in our healing community have a variety of gifts that they generously use in the service of the rest of us: cooking, baking, tending a vegetable garden, running the tractor to cut the lawns, painting, applying their electrical or mechanical skills. I constantly hold my brothers and their intentions in my prayer.

I especially enjoy having all this time to pray that the Lord might heal the wounds I have caused my victims. We keep a list of our intentions on our altar, and we commend them especially to the Lord at each day's celebration of the Eucharist. We pray especially for the healing of our own victims and their families, for each other's victims, and for all children who have ever been abused by clergy. We also pray for the healing of those whose anger against clergy abusers is frequently portrayed in newspapers, on radio, and on TV. I carry this prayer through my entire day.

I find that prayer helps me live the first three steps of the Twelve-Step program of the various Anonymous recovery programs: admitting my powerlessness, believing in a Power greater than me, and turning my life over to that Power, God. It helps me acknowledge and live the fact that there is one God, and it ain't me! Now that God is in control, I'm at peace and I'm not hurting anybody. This is quite a change from the mess I made when I tried to be in control. I don't know how I survived without acknowledging that God is the one in charge.

I'm grateful to God for the place God has taken in my life. I know all the good that has happened is through the power of God. I constantly live what St. Paul said, that we can't even say the name of Jesus without the power of the Spirit. On a shelf in my room, I have a statue of St. Francis of Assisi embracing the body of Jesus hanging on the cross. He embraced Jesus with the deepest love. I embrace him, too, in the cross clasped in my hand, but his blood still flows in his members whom I have mangled.

I am also reminded of these members as I pray the Sorrowful Mysteries of the rosary. As I think of the Lord being tormented in the garden, scourged at the pillar, crowned with thorns, carrying his cross, and hanging on it for three hours before he died, I remember that I have personally done this to children and teens in his body, the victims whom I have abused.

I deeply miss seeing my mom, who is in her nineties and in very fragile health. I call her a couple times a week and constantly urge her to hang in there and hit a hundred. We both enjoy these calls, and I am glad to be able to keep her in my prayers.

I fear some bishops and provincials have lost sight of the possibility of change and growth through prayer and therapy. My addiction can never be cured, but it can and is being controlled. By God's grace and the skill of therapists, I am no longer a person who is about to abuse a minor. Yet I feel like I am still being dealt with as a dangerous predator.

Fortunately, I haven't had to deal with the legal system or the press outside of a civil suit and a couple of newspaper articles. The articles were embarrassing for my family and disillusioning for my friends, but they brought things out into the open.

My therapeutic team for the past four years has been most understanding, encouraging, and compassionate. Through them the Lord has helped me control my addiction so that there has been no sexual activity at all for the past five years. They have helped me handle my depression, which at times

has been severe. Now we are working on helping me understand, live with, and control the anger with which I am still
seething. This anger is deeply rooted in me going all the
way back to the rejection I experienced in my childhood,
and even now, in my religious community. It is most gratify-
ing and helps to heal my wounded anger when my religious
superiors show interest in and contribute to my healing.

I can only again express my deepest sorrow and regret
to my victims and their families. I cannot ask for forgiveness, knowing that would lay a further burden on them.
I pray constantly for the Lord's infinitely powerful touch in
their lives.

Ψ COMMENTARY

This story is significantly different from the others in
some ways and, therefore, at first glance rather puzzling.
There is no history of having been sexually abused or
traumatized as a child. The author comes from a very
loving, close family, very different from the dysfunctional,
wounded, and wounding families described in the other
stories. Yet he too ends up becoming a priest who abuses.
How did this develop in this otherwise dedicated priest's
life?

Surprisingly, some of the origins of his compulsive sexual offending behaviors may come from his very happy
family background. There are hints in his description
of his childhood of feeling special, which can lead to
the thought distortions of entitlement and rationalization
that sometimes underlie sexual offense. Paradoxically, and
more important, the very closeness of his family may have
been one of the key factors in the development of his

abusive behavior. We hear haunting echoes throughout this priest's story of his deep yearning to replicate the closeness and acceptance he felt in his family and his inability to do so in his adult relationships. This becomes the core dynamic behind his sexually abusive behavior. He has a deep desire for emotional connectedness and intimacy with no outlets for this desire. It eventually becomes sexualized in a very abusive way.

Addiction Commonalities

Parallel to the other stories, there is an original childhood trauma here as well, though in this case it is not sexual. It is the ongoing trauma of feeling excluded by his peers. This ongoing experience of rejection fires inner rage, shame, and hurt, which makes him difficult to live with even when he joins a religious community. He continues to feel excluded as an adult, an exclusion now at least partially or unconsciously of his own making. He never feels accepted by his religious community and perceives himself to be in a fringe position there as well.

In addition there is the serious issue of his stunted psychosexual development, which is an almost universal characteristic of sexual abusers. He starts his religious formation at a young age and enters a high school seminary (a practice common then, very uncommon now). At this early age, he is deprived, because of the restrictive seminary environment, of ordinary interactions with other teens. This suppression of experience heightens his sexual interest and fantasy and connects it with young males his (then) age, his peers from whom he has always felt excluded and from whom he desires acceptance. This desire for closeness and acceptance becomes excessively sexualized and connected with early teen boys. He remains psychosexually fixated or stunted at this age. Due to celibacy and his psychosexual blocks, he never grows beyond this.

The author describes a very full, productive, and satisfying life as a priest. Yet below the surface there is a growing addiction similar to what we have seen in the other stories. There is the deep desire for closeness to families and to be accepted. His attraction to the boys in these families grows unchecked. He acknowledges that what he thought was love had grown into manipulation for his own gratification. He was inappropriately satisfying his desire for physical touch and closeness. He was manipulating an imaginary acceptance into the circle of his childhood peers through being emotionally close and sexual with the boys. He admits also that, when he was sexually abusing, he was acting out his anger with an element of vengeance for being excluded. Sexual abuse, or other sexual compulsions, is often not primarily about sex. It is about unmet needs for closeness and acceptance. It frequently possesses an element of anger or rage. It is really a misdirected, unconscious attempt to remedy some childhood trauma, that is, the phenomenon of trauma repetition.

As in the other stories, we see the gradual crossing of healthy boundaries, remaining at first nongenital: too much time alone with the boys, sharing a room, a tent, a back rub, a tickling contest. Because the sexual addiction was not being addressed, this progression of crossing boundaries inevitably led to genital fondling with alcohol playing a part in lowering inhibitions. Once this threshold was crossed, the sexual addiction escalated and it became increasingly enticing and compulsive to continue this abuse.

Again in this story we hear of the priest's desire to stop his compulsive abusive behavior, and his inability to do so on his own. At some level within him he knew that what he was doing was very harmful to the young men and that he was out of control. He made an attempt to control his behavior by changing his ministry to a preaching ministry that kept him always on the move from parish to parish and away from the young men that he had become overly close to. This is often referred to as the "geographical cure." In this case, it partially worked. He was mostly away from the situations that triggered his sexually abusive behavior and so the frequency of the abuse declined. Yet there were still some dangerous situations in which he was sexually abusive again. This was because he was still not facing the underlying addiction and was trying to control it on his own. It is rarely possible to stop any compulsive disorder or addiction, no matter how destructive to others and to oneself, by one's one power.

Addictions Are Unpredictable

People often ask, "How can a priest (or a minister, rabbi, father, or uncle for that matter) continue to function, often seemingly effectively, in his spiritual role and be committing such abusive sexual behavior, especially with children?" This author provides us with at least a partial answer. He describes himself as feeling generally close to God. Yet his relationship with God was "split." He compartmentalized his addiction, this compulsive desire to be sexual with young men, walling it off from the rest of his spiritual life and relationship with God. Because of shame, denial, and the addiction's power, he could not let God penetrate into that corner of his life and confront his behavior. This is common for all addicts of any kind. They eventually let no one, including themselves or God, into this shame-filled place in their brains and souls. At times, this priest could let the walls down and ask God for help about the compulsion. Eventually his prayer was answered when two fathers of his victims confronted him and he began his process of recovery.

His recovery today involves a life focused on contemplative prayer in his supervised recovery community (which includes ongoing individual and group psychotherapy). Much of his prayer is offered for the healing of his victims, their families, and his family and for all those hurt by his addictive, abusive actions. He is very eloquent in his story in expressing his sorrow for what he has done and in his empathy now for his victims. He is, as he describes, a very feeling man. So he feels deeply what he has done to his victims. He also feels deeply the losses in his family and in his ministry that his addiction created. This has cost him periods of deep depression, from which he has now emerged. He still struggles with the core anger from his rejection trauma, and he is aware of it and working on it.

We can hear some of this old anger, although perhaps some of it is just and healthy, in his complaint against some bishops and provincials. He believes that they still treat him as a dangerous predator and do not see in him and others like him the possibility of change and growth. He believes his addiction is under control and that he is no longer a threat to abuse young men. In this he raises a key and difficult issue: how does the church, and our society as a whole, need to respond to child sexual abusers who are in recovery?

My assessment of this man is that he is in very good, ongoing recovery from his sex addiction and compulsion. He is therefore at low risk for reoffending or abusing. However, the difficulty is that we cannot say that there is no risk. In fact, our ability to predict future risk with this compulsion or any other addiction is quite limited. So, I believe that we have to come down on the side of caution and of protecting children. In the wrong circumstances even this well-intentioned and well-recovering priest, and others like him, could reoffend and again hurt the innocent and vulnerable. I believe that removal from active ministry and supervised recovery communities such as the one he belongs to is generally the necessary response.

Still, his cry for understanding needs to be heard. As a church and as a society, we need to drop our judgments and vengeful anger and come to see these men as our wounded brothers, especially those who, like this priest, are working so hard to overcome their addiction and past behavior. Will God accept anything other than compassion, understanding, and forgiveness from us? Does he not call us to respond in the God-like fashion of this author's mother, who upon hearing of his abusive behavior said to him, "I know what you've done and know how wrong it was, but you are my son and I'll never stop loving you"?

Six

A PRIEST
LOOKING FOR GOD

Recently on a Greyhound bus, a middle-aged woman sat down next to me. After a few miles, she asked me what kind of work I do. I told her I was a priest, and she asked what I thought of the publicity about clergy abuse. I told her I thought it was just the tip of the iceberg. I hoped it would encourage thousands of people who had suffered abuse to come forward and tell their stories. She said she hoped so too. She went on to tell how she had been abused from childhood by her own father. She hated her mother because she believed her mother always knew yet would not interfere. She went on to tell of her numerous marriages and divorces, of all her guilt and thoughts of suicide.

Whether sexual abuse is more common now or has always been a secret that people have carried, I do not know. I do know its effects make lives miserable, and I know many people hold stories that need to be told.

As for me, I grew up in an unusual home. Both my parents were college graduates. They married during the Depression. My dad was a chiropractor, and my mother was a social worker. My mother's family was probably the most financially successful family in our town. My grandfather, however, had suffered much while living with my grandmother, who was probably bipolar. He was an outstanding Catholic. Back in the days when mostly women went to daily Mass, he was always there. He had a deep devotion to the Sacred Heart and made sure roses were before the statue when in season. When my grandfather died, I was thirteen. He was waked at home for two nights, and family after family came, recalling how he had gotten them through the Depression. He was my vocational ideal. I thought the mantle he wore was now passed on to me.

My own mother was a troubled woman. I loved her, but I denied for many years that she needed psychiatric help. I always told my relatives that they just had to get to know her. I remember one incident when my younger sister did not come home as quickly as my mother expected. When my sister arrived, a few minutes late, my mother grabbed her by the hair and rubbed her head across the wainscoting wallboard. I watched, saying nothing, horrified. After many years, my family and I came to realize we grew up in a zoo. My mother refused to get professional help, fearful, I suspect, that she would be institutionalized as her mother had been. Years later after my father died, we did have to send her to a mental hospital for a few months.

My father was a handsome, educated gentleman who lived in my grandfather's shadow. During the Depression, his practice as a chiropractor was not earning enough money for rent, so he became an accountant working long hours, taking him away from us. He never could meet my mother's expectations. When I was a teenager he drank excessively while my mother spent much of her inheritance raising eight children. After we had all left home, he began to earn incomes far surpassing their needs. Later, we saw a new side of him when my mother began to have seizures from a brain tumor. He wholeheartedly devoted himself to her, and even on his deathbed he was worrying about her.

When I was three years old, I waited for hours at the living room window for my dad to come home. I vividly remember asking myself why I was waiting there, while my older and younger sisters were playing. When he finally drove in, I ran out to meet him. Getting out of the car, he yelled at me to get out of his way. He shoved me to the side. Confused, I turned and watched my older sister run out with her arms outstretched. He picked her up, hugged her, and carried her up onto the porch where my mother and younger sister were rejoicing to see him. I stood outside watching. I felt profoundly rejected. Over the years I never connected with him. I have three younger brothers, and I remember being seven and watching him having fun with them playing on his lap. I was asking myself, "What is wrong with me?"

One time when I was about eight, my dad surprised me by taking me to a county fair, along with a friend of his. I felt singled out and glad to be with him. But at the fair, he said nothing to me. I was running to keep up with him. His friend asked, "How about lunch?" My dad said nothing and moved on. His friend bought me a foot long, and I gratefully received it. Afterward, I felt puzzled about my father's behavior toward me. Perhaps he did not have the money, but his ignoring me confused me.

WALKING IN DESOLATION

We lived on the outskirts of a small village. My grandparents lived across our driveway, and behind us, a good football field distance away, were renters on my grandfather's farm. The rumor was that they had syphilis in their family. One day as a six-year-old, I was walking home from school and the town tough, about seven years older than me, from the family who lived on my grandfather's farm, suddenly appeared kneeling on the sidewalk, stopping me. He looked directly into my eyes and started to fondle me. He seemed to come out of nowhere. Often when I was alone chopping wood, pitching down hay from our hayloft, or in our outhouse, he would appear. I never could understand why my grandmother or some other family member didn't see him. He began giving me oral sex, and at times he tried to force me to give him oral sex. I never told anyone. When I was nine, he raped me and told me to tell no one. I thought, "How could I? Here I am, a member of a privileged family, and I have been contaminated by someone who has syphilis in his blood." Emotionally I shut down, and, for the next sixty years, I felt like I was a pariah. He raped me two other times. Another time when I was feeding our cow, he was about to come into the small shed. I had a pitchfork. He knew not to come near. I wanted to thrust it into his chest.

For a considerable time, I walked in desolation. There was no one that I could trust to reveal what had happened to me. I began to think that only those who have experienced such an ordeal could ever understand anyway. My heart goes out to anyone who has been molested. No amount of money can ever take away the pain a victim carries. Part of the consequence of being abused was a transformation of my whole being. I tried to describe it in confession. I told the priest I had committed adultery. He was so upset I feared saying anything more. I felt alone, abandoned by God, and I was an angry kid. I was mean to my siblings and withdrew into myself. I became silent, began to stutter, and felt like a festering sore.

As a youngster I used to go for walks in the country and developed an intimate relationship with Jesus Christ. I wanted to give him my life, follow him, whatever the cost. When I was in high school, I read the lives of many saints. I especially admired the life of Peter Claver. For forty years he dedicated his life to the slaves who came in on ships to a port in South America. I wanted to imitate him.

My high school years were difficult. I never developed any close friends. We lived a good ten miles from the city. I started driving a car and took carloads of girls to movies or the teenager hangouts. Sexually, I was attracted to older men. I started to masturbate, but I never acted out with anyone.

In college I fantasized about being with older men who would hold me. I would go window shopping and hoped someone would stop and ask me to go with them. Three times I met men whom I followed and who gave me oral sex. I never found anyone who gave me what I desired. I applied for the seminary and was accepted. Afterward another man picked me up and forced me to have anal sex. I felt used and ashamed that I let myself be violated again. I entered the seminary and discovered I had brought crabs with me. I told the housing director I had stayed in a cheap motel on the way and must have picked them up there. He never asked any questions and got me the powder to kill them. I feared that I had entered religious life under false pretenses. I told my major superior and he told me to let go of these disturbing fears.

During my years of training I had some attractions toward a few of my peers, but I never acted out with any of them. I thought that they could not have experienced any of the sleazy life I had known. Our director of formation taught early in the training that homosexuality was not an impediment to religious life, and I never was bothered that I had these inclinations. If there was any inappropriate sexual behavior in the seminary, I never knew about it.

A PERSONAL THEOLOGY

While I was in training, I began to read every book I could find on spiritual experience. I was convinced I lived in union with Christ. One particular writer had a profound effect on my spirituality. He is the unknown author of *The Cloud of Unknowing*. He has a smaller work called *The Book of Privy Counseling*.[21] In this work, he instructs us to let gratitude dominate our lives. He writes that each of us is a creature who is necessarily limited. We could never be perfect; otherwise, we would be God. If we complain about who we are, we insult God. Gratitude is the only attitude that makes sense. He has a prayer that he suggested people memorize and feel in our hearts: "That which I am, and even the way I am, with all of my gifts of nature and grace, You have given me Lord, and You are all of it. I return it to You, to praise You, to help others, and myself."[22]

For the next fifty years, I meditated on this prayer. I considered that my homosexual orientation was a gift. I accepted it and wanted to use it for the glory of God.

When I was about twenty-five, I made a retreat under a wonderful missionary. He also taught us to let gratitude dominate our prayer life. He said if we want to become perfect, the fastest route is by way of gratitude. It will keep us in touch with reality, the reality that all we have is a gift. He also encouraged us to see God present in each person we meet. He suggested we become everyone's priests. In our imagination we were to go with them, praying that they accomplish the mission the Lord has given them. This retreat also had a significant impact on my relations with others.

During the years shortly before my ordination, shortly after Vatican II, a time historians call the sexual revolution, there was a lot of discussion about appropriate and inappropriate sexual behavior. Some believed that sex before marriage was permissible as long as the couple loved each other and were committed to one another. Similarly, homosexual love was considered okay if both parties agreed and each respected the other. This thinking certainly influenced me. I recognize today how misleading and disastrous such thinking was.

After ordination I went on for doctoral studies in spiritual theology. I read about men cruising and going to bathhouses, and I began to do the same. I always left those places empty and angry that I could not engage the men I met there in meaningful conversations. When therapists speak of dissociation, perhaps there is no greater example of that than in me, insanely looking for good in the wrong places. I continued to do research, but by this time the addiction had taken control of my life and I could not finish my dissertation.

When I returned to ministry I became a pastor. I loved the assignment. I lived in a residence hall on a university campus. I was chaplain for the college Council of the Knights of Columbus and also chaplain of a fraternity that had over a hundred men. I normally wore my clerics and wanted to be recognized as a priest. Naturally there were many attractive young adults, but I could not even conceive of acting out with any one of them. I divided the world into two groups, the good who had never been exposed to sexual abuse and the sorry lot of those who had. Because of my shame, if I had inappropriate sexual behavior with anyone, I tried to keep it anonymous.

During this period, I was living with religious men who were dedicated to Christ but were not emotionally available for one another. It was a long and lonely experience. I admit I did not give these men a fair chance. On Friday evenings the community had a social before supper. Typically I would not get away from the parish in time and would be late. I would approach the community room, look in, and be overcome with fear. I was afraid others would notice how inadequate I was. I still was under the delusion that adult men would see the flaws in me that I thought my father had.

CRUISING

Meanwhile, I heard about a lot of heavy problems from those whom I was serving, but there was no one with whom I could share my experiences. At one time, I recall I was listening to twelve penitents who were contemplating suicide. I started to cruise again and spent hours driving, rarely speaking to anyone. It was a time to numb my feelings. I kept cruising, just driving and looking. About eight years into this pattern, I began to stop and talk to young adults on the streets. I was extremely cautious. I never approached a group. I looked for someone alone, someone slender with a dark complexion, someone whose appearance indicated he took care of himself. I looked for someone who by his eyes indicated that he too was looking for a companion. I saw myself in these young men, as I had been in college, alone and wanting affection. I avoided anyone who was obviously gay. I did not want to be seen with anyone who flaunted his lifestyle.

The men with whom I talked were normally bisexual. They were married or had girlfriends, and they wanted money. I developed a deep interest in trying to understand those for whom I had an attraction. I began asking each one a number of questions: "Why are you out here? How long have you been doing this? How did you get started? Do you enjoy being on the streets? Were you abused as a child? Do you find yourself talking to God in your own way?"

Most had similar stories. They had been abused and came from dysfunctional homes. Often they were trying to make it on their own. I would drive them to a Burger King or a Taco Bell, buy them something to eat or drink. I usually feared them the first time I talked to them. Most of them feared that I was a detective. If they asked for money for sex, I told them that no amount of money could pay for what they were worth. They agreed. There were many whom I helped to get work. They often looked upon me as a father. This gave me great satisfaction. I often told them the greatest thing I could do for them was to help them deepen their faith in God. I felt good that I could have an honest and intimate conversation with them. I felt real with them; I believed I was not hiding who I really was. In retrospect, I see now I wanted intimacy, I wanted to be held, and I wanted to be with someone who could understand me. I regret I was enabling them to stay on the streets. I was using them to fill the void in my own life. What I was doing was a lie. I regret it. I pray that each of those I used will be blessed with honest and loving friends. I earnestly desire that the Lord lift them up and give them the realization that they truly are men of priceless value.

Years later, after I came back from a year of intensive therapy, a fellow addict told me, "You have to get ahold of your lust!" I thought, "Who, me? I am not led by lust!" I envisioned a lustful person as someone panting in the shadows waiting to use others for sexual pleasure. I was a friend of the men I met. I helped them. I would never engage anyone in sexual behavior who revealed that he did not want it. I was in denial that I was cultivating them. I admit, too, at times, that if a fellow did not want to be sexual, and I knew it, I often would not pick him up or help him. Lust certainly was a powerful component of my cruising.

Many times while cruising I asked myself what it was that I really wanted. Deep within, I knew it was God. Yet I feared being honest and getting help. I could not stop myself. Many times I felt the only solution was ending my life.

Those with whom I did have sexual encounters were rarely male prostitutes. Rather, they were men in their cars cruising and looking for a companion. Usually they were older than the hustlers. Many wanted to give oral sex, and they did not want to have coffee or sit and talk. I often wanted to get to know them, but this is not what they wanted. Meeting these men was rare, but the desire to do so certainly fed my addiction. Each time I was with one, I left empty and continued to cruise, searching for someone who would be personally intimate with me.

Some twenty-five years ago I picked up a hustler who was a compulsive gambler and an alcoholic. He wanted money for anal sex and I refused. We engaged in mutual masturbation. Over the next five years, he was often the only person I saw and felt safe picking up. I frequently helped him when his gambling addiction left him destitute. He got involved in a difficult marriage, and eight years ago he called and wanted me to pay for his weekly marriage counseling. I saw it as a form of blackmail and told him to talk with a priest if his past was bothering him so much. I soon learned from my superior that the man had been in touch with him. My superior asked me to go for psychological assessment. I did and began a year-long inpatient therapy program. I wholeheartedly gave myself to the program, revealing everything I experienced and remembered, deeply hoping therapy could free me.

PROVIDENTIAL MEETINGS

The compulsive gambler's disclosure was an answer to years of prayer. I knew I needed help, but I feared telling anyone. I prayed frequently that someone would see me and report me. I recognize now how insane I must have looked to the detectives and those who saw me cruising. I was scandalizing them. They knew who I was and I learned from one of them that they often laughed at me driving around the cruising area. I knew they were laughing at me, yet I insanely continued to cruise.

After six months of intensive therapy, the professionals knew my emotions were blocked but could not get to the root problem. They discussed the possibility of hypnosis and then decided against it. They asked me to try EMDR (a therapy technique).[23] I did and in the very first minutes I broke down and began crying. I was reliving the childhood rape scenario. I remembered each movement and word uttered. I had never cried about it before. At the end of the session, the therapist asked me what I would say to that child today. At first, I could say nothing. I continued to cry. Finally I said, "It's not your fault. You are not guilty." Almost miraculously, it felt like shackles around my ankles were unlocked and I was free. I had carried guilt about it for fifty years. I had thought that, since I had not resisted the perpetrator from the beginning of his abusing me, I had cooperated and had given myself up to him. I also had thought I had to deal with the abuse by myself. I remembered then how I had become emotionally bitter and hardened.

A therapist in the program helped me put my past in perspective. He told me I had three strikes against me before I got started: a bipolar mother, rejection from my father, and the traumatic sexual abuse.

After the residential program, I went back into ministry. I saw a therapist regularly, had a sponsor, and attended many Twelve-Step meetings. Despite these supports, I went back to cruising. Unfortunately, I still carried the delusion I was a pariah. Another five years passed, and a woman whose marriage I witnessed and whose husband I received into the church asked me to talk to him. They were no longer able to have sexual relations. I listened to his story. He was the youngest of three children, the oldest a brother, then a sister and he. When he was a child, his brother began to use him sexually. This continued for some years. When the brother was about thirty-three, he died of AIDS. At the funeral, the man could not cry. Asked why not, he told his sister his story, then told his wife. As he was relating his memories to me, a flash came to me: "Why, you are not a pariah!" Afterward, I asked myself why this thought had come to me. I finally realized I had been telling myself for years that I was a pariah. It was delusional thinking and had to be changed for my recovery. I was connecting it with the thought that only people who have experienced the abuse I suffered could possibly understand me. Along with lust, it was the rationalization I was using to keep cruising.

These past two years I have worked on my self-image, changing the way I perceive myself. A therapist recently told me that he had tried to change my thinking, using a crowbar. But this providential meeting with the man who shared his own story of abuse was miraculous and in a sacred moment changed my whole way of thinking about myself. I knew him and respected him. I found a good man could carry memories of being abused and still not be a pariah. When I was much younger, I often wondered what would happen to me if I kept on cruising. It was a time of fear, of desolation and emptiness. I have now begun a new chapter in my life, grateful I no longer have secrets to hide. My prayer life certainly has deepened. I especially love contemplating the Lord in nature. I enjoy watching and hearing the songs of the birds in early mornings. I love to watch the flock of geese land on the lake. I love walking through the woods with our black Labrador. I gradually am learning to clearly articulate what I am feeling. I am learning to express my anger. I am convinced that therapy and prayer do work. Occasionally, I see men whose eyes say they are looking for a companion. I say a prayer for them and I move on, pursuing what is healthy for me. I no longer need to connect with them. I cannot fill the need that they have, nor can they fill mine. I know I have been profoundly blessed and that I am a man of deep value.

Even though I do not have permission to publicly minister, I am still a priest. I could listen and empathize with the woman on the Greyhound bus. I am disappointed in the Church's response to this problem. I feel our superiors do not know what an addiction is. I feel like they are saying, "What you did was done out of malice. You made us look bad." They seem to fear the press and a loss of money. They do not understand the shame and pain addicts have suffered for years. They seem to want us to suffer more. They seem to think the best way to handle addicts is by secluding them from society. I am grateful they have given me the opportunity to have therapy. I know I still have a lot to give. I know from what I have learned from therapy and prayer that I could help other addicts who come to the confessional. I am grateful for the support and encouragement I receive from my family and friends. They are the understanding and forgiving Church. I myself am convinced that the Lord can turn our past failures into good when we entrust to him everything we are. I know an addiction can come back again, even stronger than before. For instance, I find playing spider solitaire on the computer addictive, and its effect on me is similar to cruising. It numbs my feelings. I know what I have to do to stay free and sober. I recognize that we create our freedom by planning in advance what we are to do with leisure time. In my prayer I ask the Lord for the gift of integrity, to be another Christ, who cares for self and the self of other human beings with heart and not as objects. As the retreat master encouraged us years ago, I will serve others as a priest in the image of Jesus Christ.

Thank you for listening.

Ψ COMMENTARY

After reading this last of five stories of priests who have been sexually compulsive and abusive, the pattern has probably become apparent to the reader: the adult victimizer was first, as a child, a victim of abuse. This profound trauma led to the development of a severe sexual sickness, which led to abuse, the vicious circle of abuse. This is the part of their story that is rarely captured in the media and in the public's conception of the priest sex offender. We

only get a picture of a priest or other clergy sexually mis-
behaving and being abusive or using someone sexually, in
this man's case not children, but men on the street. To
be fair to the media, the history behind these behaviors
is usually not available to them, and the priest himself
does not know the full extent of his trauma history until
it emerges in the process of psychological treatment. So
the full story remains hidden.

Too Much for a Man Alone

You, at this point, might be asking the question, Why can't
these priests just stop what they are doing, which is so
obviously wrong and abusive, especially since they are
priests and victims themselves? It is impossible to fully
get inside the mind and experience of an addict of any
kind unless you have been there yourself. Only if you have
been entrapped in the power of an addiction to alcohol or
drugs, sex, gambling, or compulsive overeating, or have
experienced severe depression, bipolar disorder, or any
serious mental illness can you really understand the control that an addiction or mental illness exerts over you.
This story provides us an inside view of sex addiction, its
power, and its origins, providing some answers as to why
these men (or any addict) could not stop their behavior
of their own volition.

We see the seeds of this priest's addiction sown first in
the painful rejection by his father very early in his childhood. In response he asks, "What is wrong with me?" He
feels closer to his mother; however, she is emotionally
unstable, unreliable, and unpredictable as a parent. Sometimes she is physically abusive, probably due to untreated

bipolar disorder. An already deeply hurting and vulnerable little boy is further traumatized and terrorized by being brutally sexually abused by a neighbor young teen and town bully from age six till he is at least nine. Like many children in his position, he cannot tell anyone who could rescue him. He is paralyzed by shame and fear and holds this awful secret for fifty years. He does go to a priest in confession, and in his childhood innocence he describes what is happening to him as adultery. Sadly, the priest misses the child's deep need, and his angry response drives the child's secret further underground. Now he feels abandoned by God as well.

All of the ingredients of his later psychosexual problems and addiction were tragically in place by the time he was nine (or younger). He desperately sought closeness and acceptance. He was flooded and overwhelmed with shame, the feeling and belief he was a pariah. This intense shame blocked and misdirected his desire to connect with others. The only people he thought might understand him were those who had also been abused, who in adulthood became the objects of his addiction. His early exposure to sex was very traumatic and violent. This set up a very conflicted, shame-based, secret obsession with sex that is typical of some victims of childhood sexual abuse. All of these characteristics are a recipe for later psychosexual problems, in his case the development of a compulsive sexual disorder.

In his story we again see the development over time of what is eventually a full-blown sexual addiction. The story tragically illustrates how this addiction eventually controls these individuals, making it impossible for them to stop by their own willpower. Because of his shame and fear, the author kept his abuse and his growing problem a secret, through compartmentalization, even from himself. This allowed the addiction to grow unimpeded. There was growing fantasy, attraction, and then some sexual experiences with older men. This represented both his desires for acceptance by his father and the effect of being sexually abused by an older male.

The addiction progresses into cruising and anonymous sexual encounters. This is aided, as the author indicates, by his dissociation, a usual effect of childhood abuse. This psychological symptom of post-traumatic stress disorder involves being partially or fully disconnected from one's inner emotions and even sometimes from one's external experiences. What starts as the child's mind defending itself from the overwhelming horrors of abuse becomes in adulthood a factor that allows the sexual addiction, and in some cases sexual abuse, to develop and continue. These persons do not feel what is happening to them or what they are doing to someone else. An aspect of this dissociation, called addictive trance, can be seen in this priest's cruising behavior.[24] He spent hours in a ritual of driving around looking for men to connect with. Most of the time he did not find anyone. He was in a mentally altered, dissociated state similar to being on drugs. He was in an addictive trance.

Two other characteristics highlighted in this story help us to answer our question. It is very apparent here that what this priest was really seeking was not primarily sex. He really craved emotional and spiritual intimacy and acceptance. He is aware of this now in recovery. He was only dimly aware of it then. All sexual compulsion and even abusive sexual behavior are more about a misdirected desire for closeness and connection or anger about the lack of it. Addicts are blocked by shame and fear from learning how to really meet their relational needs. They know no other way than their addiction. This is one of the main reasons they cannot stop and why they keep repeating behaviors that they quickly regret.

Finally, there is the matter of what happens in an addict's cerebral cortex, the part of our brain that helps us reason and make decisions that direct and control our behaviors, in this case a highly educated brain that is presumably highly developed by a priest's training. First of all, his rational mind was flooded by shame and fear, which overwhelm it and render it nonfunctional at times. Then, dissociation and trance numbed it and disabled it. We see in the story, too, how the left-brain thought processes became distorted and misdirected; because of his shame about his driven behavior, he irrationally justified and excused his behavior. This developed over time into entrenched thought distortions and even delusions. All of this kept his rational mind from monitoring and controlling his behavior as it had been designed to do. Some describe this as their brain being "hijacked" by the addiction. It is an interesting side note that the author states that the changed value judgments of the sexual revolution also affected him, reminding us that even priests and other religious leaders are not immune to such cultural shifts.[25]

So here is our answer. What makes it almost impossible for the sexual compulsive, even if he is a priest or clergyman, to stop on his own is the devil's brew combination of all of the above factors: childhood trauma, debilitating

132

shame, intense fear leading to secrecy, compartmentalization and isolation, blocked and misdirected core needs,
dissociation and addictive trance, and the distortion and
disabling of the rational mind. It is difficult to comprehend
the power of all this over the individual unless you have
been there and experienced this yourself. However, these
five priest abusers have provided us with a picture of what
it feels like to be controlled by all of the dimensions of a
powerful sexual addiction and compulsion.

Discovering Empathy

Mercifully, the author's story also shows us how all of
this was reversed in recovery. His shame is gradually de-
creasing; he no longer sees himself as a pariah. His secret
has been shared with supportive people in his life. He can
connect with others emotionally, spiritually, nonsexually.
He can usually feel his emotions and feel empathy with
others, for instance with the woman on the bus, a fellow
victim of sexual abuse. He can also feel for his victims,
the men with whom he acted out his sexual addiction, and
feel remorse for using them. His mind is much clearer, the
distortions and dissociation largely gone. He can identify
people and situations that are dangerous for his recovery and make healthy decisions to avoid them. Now he
can take control and responsibility for his life even as he
paradoxically faces and accepts his powerlessness over
his addiction. His spirituality and relationship with God
now shine forth from his story. Although his ability to
function as a priest is limited as a consequence of his addiction, he is probably more profoundly a priest, now in
his seventies, than he has been his whole life.

Until about thirty years ago, most people considered alcoholics to be morally weak and defective, simply lacking the willpower to end their drinking. In those days, alcoholics were more likely to be put in jail than to receive treatment. Today, it is widely accepted that alcoholism (along with other chemical dependencies) is a disease with genetic, biological, and environmental components. Many people view priests who are caught up in the priest abuse crisis to be morally reprehensible, degraded, and criminal. These stories dramatically reveal that these men, and all who are similarly afflicted, are sick. They suffer from a severe psychosexual-spiritual compulsive illness or disorder, which is rooted in their own childhood abuse, trauma, and family and Church dysfunction. Like an active alcoholic who hurts others or even does criminal acts as the addiction progresses, these sick priests have severely hurt their victims and some have committed criminal acts. As we have said before, unhealed, hurting people hurt; wounded people wound.

Seeing these priests, and other sex offenders, as suffering from a compulsive disease or disorder does not in any way excuse their behavior. They must be stopped and held accountable. Sometimes the accountability needs to involve criminal sanctions. An alcoholic who drives drunk is sick and yet also warrants criminal sanctions. Still, as we have done as a society with alcoholics, it is time that we see these priest victim-abusers as suffering from an illness. We need to learn to understand, treat, and prevent their illness and view them and their illness with humane compassion and care. We need to see that, beneath their sickness, there is goodness, heart, and humanity. There is even priesthood and the light of the Spirit hidden below the darkness of their addiction.

There is also, as we have seen in the stories of the priests in this book, hope for their healing and recovery. It is a myth that priest sex offenders cannot be treated successfully. There will always be some priests and other sex offenders who cannot be rehabilitated. However, research has found very low rates of further abuse by clergy who have received treatment for their sickness. The relapse rate of one large group of priests treated and studied at St. Luke's Institute in Maryland was only 4.4 percent.[26] So let us not cast these men off as pariahs, as the new lepers of our society. The Francis of Assisi of our time would kiss the abuser, as the St. Francis of the thirteenth century kissed the outcast, physical leper of his time. We are invited to embrace them as our wounded and sickened brothers. They have broken their vows, they have broken our trust, they have broken the hearts of their victims, yet their hearts are broken as well. Let's focus on mending all the hearts of victim and victim-abuser alike.

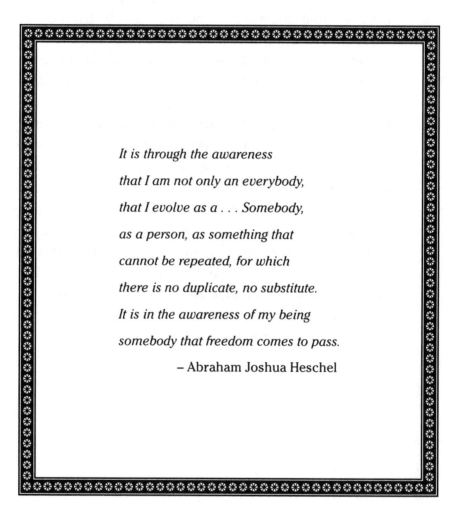

It is through the awareness

that I am not only an everybody,

that I evolve as a . . . Somebody,

as a person, as something that

cannot be repeated, for which

there is no duplicate, no substitute.

It is in the awareness of my being

somebody that freedom comes to pass.

– Abraham Joshua Heschel

HEALING AND HOPE
FOR SURVIVORS

Seven

A SURVIVOR
WHO WAS SET APART

*****

> As the deer longs for streams of water
> so my soul longs for you, O God.
> My being thirsts for God, the living God.
> When can I go and see the face of God?
> My tears have been my food day and night
> as they ask daily, "Where is your God?"
> Those times I recall as I pour out my soul.
> — Psalm 42:1–5

Vague memories of my First Communion float in my mind. I'm not sure if I actually remember it, or if a photograph taken then makes me think I remember. In my First Communion picture I am standing next to Father, our local priest, with my classmates. I am leaning into him. At age seven, the look of confidence on my face indicates the pride I had in being able to stand next to him. Several months later that happy day would be overshadowed by a tragedy of immense proportions.

I can remember that time with clarity. I see Father's presence today as he was many years ago. Father walked into the hospital room with confidence, authority, and his usual wit and powerful charisma. As a priest, he had to be the strong one, the hero for the suffering. I can remember, amid my fear, feeling a sense of comfort when he walked in. Then, I always felt comforted in his presence. He was a familiar face in a hospital full of strangers.

A GRIEVING FAMILY

It was a warm September day in 1963, and my family was involved in a terrible auto crash just a quarter of a mile from our home. Two young teenagers, out for a joy ride, ran a stop sign and careened into the side of our car, sending it rolling into a newly harvested cornfield. The local police had been chasing them. As the story is recounted to us, my mother was thrown from the car and was found lying some distance away with serious injuries. Jacob, then nine, crawled out of the car and over my little sister, Katie, six, who partially was pinned under the car. Jacob was found wandering around the cornfield. I was some distance into the cornfield, cut, bruised, and unconscious. Michael, four, was lying near the car and suffered a leg broken in several places and many cuts and bruises. Katie, pinned under the car and crushed by its weight, was dead at the scene.

We were returning from taking my Dad to retrieve his pickup truck, which had been repaired. Michael and Katie wanted to ride with him, but my father had chosen to stay in town and have a few beers with his buddies. When some-one ran to tell him that his entire family had been in a terrible crash, he rushed to the scene, and with some other men, he attempted to lift the car off Katie. I know this story because my Dad told me about it years later. A stranger stopped to help the men lift the car, and that is how they unpinned Katie. My family's emotional trauma over Katie's loss would lay the groundwork for years of vulnerability, heartache, and pain. I was told that when my mother received the news that Katie had died, a scream was heard throughout the entire floor of the hospital. It gives me chills to think of the pain that she endured in that moment, a moment that would have an impact on the rest of her life. To this day I am hypersensitive to my mother's emotions and tears.

In the mid sixties little was known about the process of grief, the stages of guilt, denial, anger, and deep pain. My mother was told to pray to God to learn to accept this tragedy. My brothers and I went home from the hospital and were told not to speak about our sister in front of our mother; it would upset her too much. By the time we got home, family members had removed everything that belonged to Katie except her school lunch box. So we remained silent about our own loss and grief for many years. My mother still has the lunch box. This dreadful experience and our personal vulnerability gave Father a clear pathway to enter our lives.

This story begins with the loss of a sibling, but moves very slowly and subtly into one of emotional and sexual abuse. I was dominated and manipulated and felt shame, guilt, and fear. I was the victim of misuse of pastoral authority, the breach of a sacred trust. But this is also the story of love, grief, healing, friendship, and forgiveness. A priest abused me and put me into servitude for fourteen years. This is a story of my journey toward wholeness. My willingness to share this story is driven by a hope that other women who have been victimized by the overwhelming abuse of power within the Catholic Church might finally have a voice, a voice that is long overdue for women in the Church, for I believe our numbers are many.

141

After the crash that took Katie's life, my family did its best to return to some semblance of normalcy. I remember my grandparents and aunts spending a lot of time at our house. Our home was a very sad one for a long time. I don't have vivid memories of my own grief in the days after the accident. Other than remembering Father's visit to me in the hospital, my only other clear memory is being driven to the funeral home the morning of Katie's funeral. My mother was still hospitalized with serious injuries and couldn't attend. We children weren't able to attend the funeral either, but my aunt and uncle drove us there so my dad could see us. I can still see his face leaning into the backseat window to tell us that Katie was an angel now. Tears filled his eyes.

As our lives went on, Father made weekly appearances to visit, play, and eat ice cream with us. He was a welcome visitor; there was happiness and laughter when he came to visit. I attended religion classes each Saturday morning, and my attachment to him continued to grow. He became a second father to me, and in many ways I carried greater respect and awe for him than I did for my own father. I was too young to imagine he had a dark side. He carried such an attitude of authority with him, even though I saw how abusive he could be to people who tried to challenge him. He took pride in humiliating people in front of others.

I remember sitting in a meeting of the parish women's society as a teenager. A woman questioned something he wanted them to do as a group, and he became so verbally abusive to her that no one challenged him any further. It was always his way or no way. So I knew not to cross him for fear of being belittled in front of others. On a youth ministry mission trip, one of the teenagers accidentally broke a statue of the Sacred Heart of Jesus with a volleyball. When he found out who broke the statue, Father ordered the young man to kneel in front of the statue and confess, in front of everyone, what he had done. The obstinate young man refused. When he finally stood up in defiance, Father struck him in the face with his fist and then struck him a second time, breaking a tooth. I absolutely feared his anger. I understood, if provoked, he could be violent.

In my own early experience, the manipulation was subtle. It began when I was just seven with the demand for respect, the "Yes, Father, no, Father" responses that we were forced to say. If we failed, we were immediately reprimanded. Under the guise of respect for the "representative of Christ," we were obligated to treat priests and religious with utmost respect regardless of how inappropriate they were. Sadly, we believed Father and other clergy were without human flaw.

Father's powerful skills of manipulation were masterfully concealed behind his potent charisma. People either acquiesced to his control and followed him or quickly sized up his motives and moved away. The vulnerable were swept into his conservative theology, charismatic presence, and subtle domination. I was one of the vulnerable ones, initiated at an early age.

Throughout high school my personal involvement with the Church and with Father grew. I was eager to be involved in everything in the parish. It was a growing community, and exciting things were happening. He challenged us to put our faith into practice by volunteering our time with various parish activities, and later he encouraged us to form a youth group to reach out to the poor. All of this was exciting and fulfilling for me. He taught us weekly religion throughout high school and instilled a strong awareness of our responsibility as young Catholics to make a difference in the world. It sounds like a positive message, doesn't it? And it was! The undercurrent, though, was that he had been reeling me into his control since age eight. No one, including me, saw it happening. By my teenage years, he had created an allegiance to him that would be extremely difficult to defy and break. I would have done anything he asked me to do.

LOOKING UP TO A MAN

One incident started a pattern of sexual abuse. I had just graduated from high school and was attending a small college not far from my home, and Father offered me a part-time job in our small parish as his secretary. The little office he gave me was just outside the sacristy. After Mass one morning, I was sitting at my desk working when he emerged from the sacristy. There was a step up into the sacristy, so when he appeared in the doorway, I looked up at him and noticed immediately that he had an erection. I remember quickly turning away to get busy about my work, not wanting to acknowledge what I had just seen. I also remember feeling very confused about what that meant. After all, he had just come out of Mass; why would that be happening now? I was eighteen and had some knowledge of sex, but not enough to explain what I had just seen, especially from a priest.

Several weeks went by without incident until late one afternoon as I was leaving the office to go home. I was still living with my parents at that time, and we always ate dinner around 5:30 p.m., so I was anxious to get home. He met me as I was walking out of the office. We stopped and talked for a few minutes. Acting tired and sad, he reached out for me and pulled me to himself and began kissing me. It lasted only a few seconds, but it was his entrée into a pattern of sexual abuse he would perpetrate against me for the next fourteen years. I had been trained never to question, never to judge what Father said or did. I had learned that lesson very well, and when the abuse started I was not capable of identifying that what was happening to me was inappropriate and abusive on many levels. Among several chaotic thoughts and questions, the predominant feeling was that I had been "set apart," that I had become someone very special and important to him.

The kiss and embrace were only the beginning, and within weeks it led to him taking my hand and placing it on his penis and him touching my breasts. From there, it moved into complete nudity and sexual gratification for him. There was never any sexual mutuality. There was never intercourse, only my oral or hand masturbation of him. He discouraged me from taking any action that would get me aroused. My sexual arousal seemed to frighten him. I believe he felt that if he kept me from becoming too aroused, his guilt would be less. This attitude was consistent with the clerical culture in which he was formed: women, the temptresses, are to be kept under control lest they take control. This attitude led me into a life of indentured sexual servitude to him from 1975 until 1989. I was never allowed to call him by his first name, only Father. One day I asked him if I could call him by his first name, and with great indignation he responded by saying, "Absolutely not!"

In *Is Nothing Sacred?* Marie Fortune explains, "Consent to sexual activity, in order to be authentic, must take place in the context of mutuality, choice, full knowledge, equal

145

power and in the absence of coercion and fear. When there is an imbalance of power in a relationship these necessary factors will not be present."[27] We were not peers, nor were we equals, and the consent was not authentic; it was not consent at all. He was sixty years old when the abuse began. I was eighteen. I have struggled with my own culpability in this unhealthy relationship. The reality is that I was a young adult and I could have said no, yet there was so much more involved than my ability to say yes or no to the relationship. From the time I was a small child, I had never been able to say no to him.

The control he had over my life was overwhelming. There was little other focus in my life but his work, his ministry. Two years after I began working for him, he encouraged me to discontinue my university studies. He had lofty plans to build a retirement community adjacent to the parish, and he saw a significant place for me in the development of this center. It sounded like an opportunity not to be missed. So amid the sexual abuse, I was being offered a bright and sound future in development and administration. It was an exciting time, and I felt an integral part of it all. Not only did he have in me a sexual slave, but he also had begun the process of grooming me to fulfill his vision of creating the center. I stepped up to the plate and committed myself to making "his" dream come true. And it did come true.

My first awareness that something was not right in my life began in 1981. I was twenty-four and confused about who I was. I felt unsettled, anxious. The stress of holding this shameful secret so tightly was beginning to take a toll on my emotional life. I knew I was living a clandestine and dual existence. His expectations of me continued to be very demanding. Even though I knew the sexual relationship with

146

him was morally wrong, I could not remove myself from him. At that time I did not understand that his desire to have sex with me was a breach of trust in the most grievous way. Nor did I understand that he was playing the role of surrogate father to me, thus making the sexual abuse incestuous. His constant affirmation of me and his expectations kept me in his servitude. It was all I had ever known. I remember lying in bed at night thinking that I had to do something; I just didn't know what to do. This dysfunction and aberration in my life led me to binge drinking with my peers. Desperately wanting to fit in, I would drink excessively on weekends and then fall back into his control during the week.

A PROFOUND EXPERIENCE

The one thing I felt for sure was that I had a deep call to serve the poor and a strong desire to experience the poor outside the United States. This missionary spirit within me was an early gift that I had identified within myself. Mother Teresa of Calcutta was becoming well known at that time. Malcolm Muggeridge's book *Something Beautiful for God* was very popular.[28] I was taken by the stark poverty of the people whom Mother was serving in India. I wanted to experience this poverty. Now, I realize that my draw to Mother Teresa was a response to the incredible emotional poverty in my own life at that time. I didn't know this then, but in retrospect, I can look back and see my intense need to flee the sexual servitude in which I was living. I couldn't find another way out of what was happening to me, and the thought of reaching out for help was out of the question. Who would I trust with this secret?

I left for India to the great dismay of my family and Father. I stayed there only two and a half months, having to return early because of an illness. What happened to me there was profound. I saw people left to die in the streets from disease and malnutrition. Daily we went out to pick up those who had collapsed on the streets and brought them to the Home for the Dying so they could die with some shred of human dignity. We visited a leper colony each week and took food and medicine. I saw human beings who were dying because of lack of food and medicine. I experienced the poorest of the poor in India for the first time. I learned how to integrate faith and action; I learned to see Christ in the poor; I began to understand a global spirituality.

When I returned home from India, nothing with Father really changed. I resumed my employment at the parish and with the center he was developing. To cope with the abuse I immersed myself in work, putting in sixteen- to eighteen-hour days. The abuse continued throughout my workdays. He would come into the office while I was working late or invite me to his rectory. There was always another reason for going to his rectory, helping him clean or going over some notes from a meeting or having a late dinner. I was drifting on a raft of denial.

What did change, though, was my worldview. My experience in India with Mother Teresa's community opened my eyes to an expansive world, to an awareness of other ways to use my gifts, and to serious issues of social justice. In 1984, I was invited to serve in a leadership capacity with an organization associated with Mother Teresa. I became involved with her international network, and they drew me out and gave me opportunities to move away from Father's influence. I began to see that my own giftedness was appreciated. This healthy network of people called me forth to serve in ways I had never imagined. I began attending meetings in Europe, where I played an important role. This was the first thing in my life that Father was not involved in, and it was my salvation. This involvement with Mother Teresa was an immeasurable grace to me and would be a healthy and life-giving support to me as I moved toward breaking the silence and beginning my recovery work.

TAKING STEPS TOWARD FREEDOM

During this time I sought spiritual direction from a Franciscan sister. Although I never shared my secret with her, she must have known there was something terribly wrong and recommended that I see a counselor. This suggestion both frightened me and intrigued me. I held on to the phone number for several weeks before I could muster the nerve to call. The good thing about this counselor was that her office was a fair distance from my home, so there was a semblance of safety in this distance. I remember the day I made the call. It was raining and I was in my office. I closed both of my office doors for privacy and fearfully made the call. The knot in my stomach felt like a baseball. The voice on the other end was kind and reassuring, and yes, she would be happy to see me. She congratulated me on having the courage to call her, and the first appointment was made. Thus began my journey of self-discovery.

I fearfully, gradually, bit-by-bit, revealed my story to my therapist over the next year. Having my story heard compassionately was a huge relief to me and gave me strength to seek the next steps. I knew that stopping the sexual abuse was critical in my recovery. It was several months into my counseling when I made the decision to stop the sexual abuse. Father knew I was seeing a counselor because I had to take time away from my work. He discouraged me from going, often referring to my therapist as a "kook" or a "shrink." He belittled the process in order to make me look weak. I could see that he was very nervous about my seeking help. I finally found the courage and told him that I could no longer continue the relationship with him. Before I could finish what I had to say, he became angry and started yelling at me saying that it was he who could no longer deal with our relationship psychologically.

He became enraged, shoved me up against a wall and began to attempt to have sex with me. I was able to break free from him and left immediately. This was one of my most frightening experiences with him, as I feared he would physically harm me. I could see the rage in his eyes and his fist was clenched as if he wanted to hit me. I think he knew he was losing control of me. It reminded me of the times when he would be ready to ejaculate and would knock me off of the bed or frantically push me away.

Later, In processing these episodes with my therapist, she identified this action as rape. I was shocked to hear her say it, as my vision of rape was a more brutal physical battering and more violent intercourse. But all of what he had done to me was rape in the larger sense of the word. It was the total rape of my life, diminishing my own personal power, using me for his personal and sexual gain. The word "rape" was difficult to hear and process. I began to look at the issues that rape victims have to deal with and found they were similar to my own experience and process of healing. This particular aspect of the story has been the most painful to acknowledge. Like most rape victims, I, too, was afraid to break the silence and afraid no one would believe me.

Almost a year after the sexual relationship ended, I attempted a futile dialogue with him about why he allowed the abuse to go on for so long. His response was, "I thought I was helping you; I thought you needed it." What exactly did I need? To be used and discarded by him? Did I need him to control every aspect of my life? Who gave him permission to decide what I needed? Did the thought ever occur to him to ask me what I wanted?

I was in counseling for just over a year before I had the courage to fully admit that a priest had sexually abused me for fourteen years, and then I was only able to tell my therapist by letter. No other soul had known this information, and now the silence was broken. Words cannot describe the fear, guilt, and shame I carried inside at having spoken that truth. I remember driving to St. Louis after I had sent the letter, I was filled with such anxiety that I was nauseated the entire two hours. Sadly, at the time I broke the silence, I didn't yet understand that I had been abused. I carried the shame and the guilt of the relationship as if I had initiated it and encouraged it. I believed it was my fault. I felt such shame at my inability to stop the abuse. Throughout counseling my therapist reiterated to me, "This was not your fault, the abuse began with his manipulation of you starting at age seven." It was Father who had crossed many personal boundaries in the development of our relationship. I have always wondered if he had just been waiting until I turned legal age before he made his sexual advances toward me.

From 1990 to 1993 I drove several hours biweekly for therapy sessions. The sessions were painful and grueling as I disclosed every difficult aspect of my life. It was a gut-wrenching experience to disclose such intimate information to another human being, yet I was beginning to understand that it was absolutely necessary to bring about the healing and understanding that I desperately wanted. I knew that the brainwashing I had endured under this priest had to be reversed. It was as though I had been living in a cult during those years. My therapist was gifted and experienced in working with abuse victims. She gently guided me through those difficult times, never pushing me farther than I could go emotionally. Some of those sessions were filled with more pain than I thought my heart and soul could endure. I shed buckets of tears in her office.

Facing my anger was difficult. My family dynamic did not include expressing anger. I had learned from an early age to repress my anger. I learned to pout instead of being angry. My expression of anger over my abuse had been muted. My therapist encouraged me to write what I was angry about. She encouraged me to hit a pillow with a Wiffle ball bat, or punch a pillow or scream, all in safe places. At times the hurt of it all overcomes me and I have to take out a pen and paper and write why I am angry. The list usually looks like this:

I'm angry because I was used.
I'm angry because I was abused.
I'm angry because I felt powerless.
I'm angry because I allowed it to happen.
I'm angry because he took away precious years from
 me, years when I could have fallen in love and
 begun a family of my own.
I'm angry because I placed so much trust in him and
 that trust was betrayed.

152

I'm angry at the manipulation and control.

I'm angry because I did so much for him and he repaid it with his abusiveness.

I'm angry because it has disrupted my life so much.

I'm angry at the Church for not taking responsibility for its clergy.

I'm angry at the loss I've experienced in my Catholic faith.

I'm angry because of the pain.

I'm angry because I enabled him to be successful in his endeavors.

I'm angry because he blames me.

I'm angry at his denial.

I'm angry that I lived such a lie for so long.

I'm angry at the institutional Church for being so incredibly dysfunctional.

Reconnecting with my inner child was also a significant part of my therapy. The terribly wounded child within me had a tremendous amount of healing to do. I had never grieved the loss of my sister; finally I was able to release the grief that was held back for thirty years. Understanding that I needed to grieve Katie's loss helped me understand more fully my vulnerabilities as a child, the vulnerability Father used.

Keep in mind that while I was in the thick of counseling and anger work, I continued to work for the priest who was my abuser. I still did not have the courage to break my ties with him totally. I was still living with the attitude that any gifts or abilities I had were only good within his environment. The sexual abuse had stopped, but my emotional and financial ties to him remained strong. The cultish ties to him ran deeply, and it would take time before I could be fully released.

After biweekly counseling for almost two years, I also began attending a support group for victims of sexual abuse led by my therapist. This step in the process was difficult because it meant disclosing my deep, dark secret to other people. I knew it would be done within a safe and secure environment, but the fear, the knot in my stomach, was always there. In time I learned the stories of other women who had been abused, some by priests, some by religious sisters, some by their fathers, uncles, or brothers. The issues were much the same regardless of their relationship to the woman.

There were times in this group process when all I could do was sit quietly and weep. I couldn't speak and I could barely listen, but I was there. As I proceeded through my therapy, I came to understand how much my abuser had taken from me. I came to understand how terribly violated I had been by a person who represented all that was good and holy about life and my faith. All that I had held dear was being shaken to the core; a sacred trust had been broken. By my early thirties, I had come to understand that he had taken my ability to date men and possibly marry when my peers were marrying, and my ability to have children and a family of my own. This pain was one of the deepest and most hurtful of all. I grieved the loss of all that my life could have been during those years. I became keenly aware of the barriers I had put up that kept me from entering into any relationship with another man. I felt like damaged goods. After all, who would want me after having lived this secret for so long? Those barriers are still prevalent fifteen years after the abuse stopped. It is an issue that I continue to work on today.

A VALUABLE HUMAN BEING

Every other week I attended my counseling sessions and support group meeting. Between my counseling and group, I would go to an inner-city soup kitchen and volunteer my time with Mother Teresa's sisters, the Missionaries of Charity. My time there was a way to remove myself from the counseling environment, clear my head, and do some good for someone else. It always felt good to spend time on things that weren't so self-focused. Mother Teresa's missionary efforts around the world continued to play a big role in my life. In January 1991, Mother Teresa invited me to serve in a leadership capacity for a lay movement that supported her work in the United States. The invitation from her came at a time when I was emotionally destitute. It was relatively early in my counseling process, and I was just beginning to realize the full impact of the abuse I had endured. One afternoon after counseling, I proceeded to drive to the soup kitchen for my volunteer stint. I was still discerning what my response to Mother's invitation should be. Entering the sisters' small chapel, I was drawn to lie on the floor in front of the crucifix in search of an answer. In the early days of my four years of counseling there were times when I felt I couldn't go on. I struggled with suicidal thoughts, wanting to run into bridge abutments on the interstate on my way to counseling. I was terribly depressed and felt completely depleted. Now I asked God two questions, How on earth can I possibly say yes to Mother Teresa's request at this time in my life? And how could I ever say no to this woman whom I have come to revere and love so much?

Ultimately I said yes, believing that God would give me what I needed to meet the demands placed on me in this volunteer position. Just as my experience in India ten years before had opened up a whole new world for me, this invitation from Mother expanded my worldview even further. I attended many meetings with Mother Teresa from 1986 to 1994. My life played a small role in her life, but she played a huge role in mine. My association with her gave my life purpose and a sense of belonging to something so much bigger than myself.

In 1992, during a particularly dark time, my therapist suggested that I write to Mother Teresa to request some private time to share my story with her. My first reaction to her suggestion was that it would never happen. However, I knew that Mother was coming to Washington, D.C., and the more I thought about it, the more I felt drawn to contact her. I sent a simple telegram to Rome saying that I would like an opportunity to meet privately with Mother when she was in Washington regarding a personal matter. To my surprise I received a response from Rome within just a few days, and a time and place was set for the meeting. Mother's health was beginning to fail at this time. I remember how gray her complexion was and how exhausted she appeared. When she entered the room where we met, I remember feeling a bit guilty at having added this to her schedule. In her quiet humble way she entered the room and came to me with her hands folded in the traditional Bengali namaste greeting; she took my hands in hers and invited me to sit with her. I began crying and she touched my hand as we sat for a few minutes together. Then, I simply explained that for many years a Catholic priest had sexually abused me, that it had stopped and I was beginning both to heal and to grieve the loss of so much in my life. She listened quietly. The first thing she said was, "We must pray for our priests. We must trust and have confidence that Jesus walks with us through everything, that our suffering was his suffering first." She also said something I had heard her say so often before, "When we are suffering so much, it is Jesus that is kissing us. We may want to tell Jesus to stop kissing us, but he knows it is the way to holiness." I understood from Mother that I should trust that the one who loves me the most has already suffered my pain and knows it. We cannot know hope without struggle and pain. She encouraged me to trust! From the first time I met Mother Teresa, I felt wrapped in her sacred healing light and even more so after this visit. My involvement with her was a safety net that kept me from falling into a deep chasm.

As the months progressed and I continued my counseling, I could feel myself getting stronger. The new knowledge that I gained was empowering me. My therapy was retraining my mind and attitude about myself. My therapist opened me up, and affirmed I was a competent, lovable, valuable human being. My confidence grew, and I thought about taking steps to ensure that Father was held accountable. He was no longer sexually abusing me, but his emotional and verbal abuse continued and I resisted every episode. I wasn't strong enough to leave his employment yet, but I was digging in my heels and saying "no" to the emotional abuse.

In 1993, after having been in counseling for three and a half years, I broke the silence with my family, some select friends, and eventually the diocese. My parents were shocked and angered to hear the news that Father had been abusing me for so long. They knew of his control over my life but never imagined it was sexual, too. They didn't have much to say verbally, but I knew they believed me and that they supported me. Remember anger was not an emotion that my family openly displayed. They still belonged to his parish, so it was difficult for them to face him and not say anything to him. I told each of my siblings separately. All had experienced emotional abuse by him, too. My father had a stroke and a heart attack less than a year after I broke the news to him. I'll never know whether it was due to his intense anger or not; however, my instinct tells me it was related. Around the same time, I had also gone to the vicar for priests in our diocese to break the silence officially to him.

Going to the diocese was a huge step for me. It was made only slightly easier because the vicar for priests was a priest I had known and respected for many years. Driving to his parish several miles away from my home, I had to pull over twice to vomit. I went alone; it was something I had to do on my own. He received me warmly, and his gentle, quiet presence calmed my frayed nerves. I explained my experience with Father, and in addition presented a folder of documentation about his financial misuse of parish funds. I thought that if they wouldn't remove him because of the sexual abuse, they surely would because of his financial mismanagement of Church funds. The priest assured me he would take this information to the bishop, and he asked if I would be willing to meet with officials of the diocese as well as their accountants for more detailed questioning. I agreed and waited for their call. During this time and as I progressed through my process with the Church, this priest would be the only one who treated me with respect and acted with integrity.

Although my years of counseling had empowered me, my newfound confidence was sorely tested in this next phase of my recovery work. To challenge an institution as large as the Catholic Church was something I had never dreamed of having to do. By now, I had a small group of friends who gave me tremendous support. In the months to come, I would need their support more than ever. It was a frightening time. My neighbors informed me that they had seen Father behind my house late at night. I felt unsafe in my own home. He was stalking me. I learned much later that, while I was away visiting a friend in Phoenix, he had a locksmith unlock my house under the guise of looking for some paperwork that he needed. He was clearly nervous about what might happen next, and my fear of him grew.

I met with our bishop on two occasions. During the first meeting he asked me what I needed. I said I had incurred thousands of dollars in counseling costs; was there any way the diocese could help me recoup some of those expenses? He assured me that the diocese would do whatever it could to help me. Right there he wrote me a check for three thousand dollars and asked that I provide an itemized list of my costs over the last four years and submit them to him. He expressed gratitude for the information I had provided the diocese. I met with the bishop a second time to deliver my itemized list of costs for counseling. It was a cordial visit without much substance. This bishop had publicly acknowledged he was alcoholic. I smelled alcohol on his breath and saw him weave awkwardly when he entered the room. He seemed almost incoherent. I thought it would probably be the last time I would see him about this abuse issue. My instinct was correct.

I waited several weeks for a response from the bishop, but to no avail. I contacted the vicar for priests. He informed me that they had brought Father, my abuser, into the chancery office for an interview about the abuse. I was told that he had been verbally reprimanded for the abuse and the financial mismanagement. He was removed as pastor of the parish and given the opportunity to retire. Within a few weeks of this meeting, Father announced at a Sunday liturgy that he was retiring and this would be his last Mass in the parish. The small community of parishioners was shocked by this announcement.

The diocese had been kind enough to orchestrate the announcement of Father's retirement from the parish while I was to be in Africa. Before I left, though, I told a board member from the center where I worked that Father was about to be removed from the parish. When I returned home from Africa, he asked if I would be willing to meet with him and the center's attorney. I said yes, and a meeting was set. It was obvious he was concerned that I might file a sexual harassment claim against the center.

Returning home from Africa to chaos in our small community was another frightening experience. I was still employed by Father's organization, and it would take a full year yet to leave. The wrath I experienced from him was horrible. He couldn't terminate my employment with the center, but he could make my life miserable and did. A woman who was employed at the center who had been a great support to me was fired for no reason. I knew I was going to have to leave, but financially I was fearful of my ability to support myself at that time. Rumors were flying. Word was out that I had gotten the good Father removed from the parish. I was labeled mentally ill, psychologically imbalanced, crazy, a liar.

It went on for months. Father had sickly twisted and shifted the culpability to me. This is a common thread for all victims of sexual abuse. "The blaming of the victim inadvertently admits the truth of the allegations," Marie Fortune wrote in *Is Nothing Sacred?*[29] The truth was out, but many could not accept it.

I met the board member and the board's attorney after returning from Africa. Their immediate questions were, "How long has this been going on?" "Why did you decide to say something now?" "Did you have sexual intercourse with him?" "Was there penetration?" With that final question, I stood up and walked out, never to speak to them again. It was a humiliating experience, and I felt revictimized by their callous questioning and arrogance.

By now it was late 1993, and the diocese had cut off all communication with me. After multiple attempts to communicate with the bishop regarding my counseling costs, I was given the silent treatment. This infuriated me, so I began the process of finding an attorney to represent me. This proved to be an equally challenging experience, as Father was well known and loved by many people. After painstakingly revealing my story to four local attorneys, I gave up. I contacted SNAP (Survivors Network of those Abused by Priests), and they referred me to an attorney out of state. Within a few months a letter of demand was sent to the diocese, and by late June 1994, a settlement was reached. My intention to take legal action was never about the money. It was about holding the Church accountable for the abuse I had suffered.

On the day of the settlement closing I walked into the office of the diocesan attorney, whom I knew. He knew my abuser well also. He barely made eye contact with me. The $91,000 settlement agreement I was about to sign included a "no-fault clause." They were agreeing to this settlement without accepting any fault for what happened. I could never sue them again, and I could never publicly disclose any information about this case. It was a gag order, and I knew it. I just wanted it to all be over so I could move on with my life, continue my healing, and build a new life for myself. I cried quietly throughout the proceedings. My attorney asked me if I had a problem with what I was signing, and I said, "It feels like he's thrusting his penis down my throat again." The room was silent, and we quickly finished so I could leave. I sat in the parking lot for at least thirty minutes and wept alone.

AFTERMATH

Other than losing his parish and a slight humiliation in having been confronted by the bishop, my abuser was not really held accountable for his behavior. The Catholic Church wields tremendous power. Priests are rarely held accountable for grievous offenses unless word is broken to the media and they are forced to respond. How many women in the Church today have suffered the same abuse of power that I did? I believe our numbers are legion. If the bishops who manage and oversee the work of their priests had to survive in the corporate world they would never make it. Their incompetence in dealing with problem priests causes immense harm to the people they are expected to serve. My abuser had been a problematic leader for many years with no intervention from the diocese. Even they were afraid of him.

I finally had the freedom to resign my position at the center after seventeen years of employment. It was all I had ever known. Father's parting words to me on the last day of my employment were, "You'll never amount to anything away from here." What he really meant is that I wouldn't be anything without him. I did not lay eyes on him again. He continued in ministry at the retirement center he had developed and died there in late 2003.

After I left my job in 1994, I took some much-needed time off. I felt such an incredible sense of loss, and although I didn't have to worry about an income for several months, for the first time in my life I had no idea what I would do with myself. My identity had always been with Father, the parish, and the center. I moved to a small community and began to think of a new life for myself.

Through my involvement with Mother Teresa I had become close to her community of religious brothers who worked in inner-city Los Angeles, so I went to spend time with them and immerse myself in their world with the poor and homeless. This was the best thing I could have done for myself. It was healing for me to work with the poor and suffering again, and it reminded me how incredibly blessed and surrounded by love I was. In the larger picture my problems seemed to be very small compared to theirs. As justified as my own personal sorrow was, it was clearly time for me to move on and keep my experience in perspective. I was being called away from my own self-focus and the calling was coming from deep within me.

Macrina Wiederkehr, OSB, speaks these words of wit and wisdom in her book *Behold Your Life*:

Imagine that you are standing before the door of whatever tomb you've sealed yourself into. Listen to the voice of a friend calling out to you,

I called you through your door,
"The mystics are gathering
in the street. Come out!"

"Leave me alone.
I'm sick."

"I don't care if you're dead!
Jesus is here, and he wants
To resurrect somebody."[30]

Not long after I returned home from Los Angeles, I met a religious sister who wanted to create an AIDS ministry in our community. She didn't want to do the development and administrative part of the ministry, so she and I teamed up. As I became more immersed in the AIDS community, I began to learn more and more about the gay community as well. After a year in AIDS ministry, I learned that our bishop was a sexual predator of young men within the gay community. He was the same bishop I had gone to for help with my abuser. We further learned of several diocesan priests who were exhibiting similar risky sexual behavior within the community. As I began to receive this information, my level of anger at the Church escalated. I felt revictimized by the bishop. The man I had gone to for help turned out to be a sexual abuser himself.

My healing process continues even fifteen years after the abuse stopped. At one point in my process I thought that I had done all the healing work that I needed to do. However, healing from sexual abuse isn't something you manage with a few years of therapy. It is a life-long process. Sitting in church on a Sunday morning I still feel "set apart." I know things that most people sitting in the pews don't know. I wonder what they would think if they knew. How would they cope with their faith life if they had a similar experience or knew the truth of what lies behind the public lives of some of the priests whom they have put on pedestals? Would they revolt? Would they stand up and say "no more"?

My commitment to the Catholic faith wanes intermittently because of the blatant contradictions against the dignity of human life. I long to be in full communion with the faith that runs through my veins, but cannot abide the clearly antigospel behavior that comes out of the Vatican and the hierarchy, both from Rome and from local bishops. I have lost all confidence in the Church's leadership. I distrust most clergy and suspect most of what they preach is not authentic. That's not to say that it is, it's just how I feel when I hear them preach. I attend Mass when I feel it is right for me to do so. If I awaken on a Sunday morning and feel the need for Eucharist I will go; otherwise I pray quietly at home with the readings for the day. I participate in small faith communities and feed my ravenous hunger to deepen my own spiritual life through a committed life of action and contemplation. I will never follow blindly again. I will discern my own beliefs and live my faith in the way God calls me.

I became aware in recent months of my need to go back into weekly counseling after ten years. It seemed that the constant barrage of media coverage of the sex abuse crisis in the Church had affected me more than I thought. My level of anger toward the Church seems to be at an all-time high. I know that I have to find an outlet for this anger, a way to vent it before it becomes destructive within me, and before I transform my pain by transmitting it to others. A close friend said to me recently, "When a priest uses religion to imprison you, the scarring is far more profound than just the casual sexual involvement with someone else. Healing takes a lifetime because it scars the soul as well as the body and mind. I think the price you have to pay for healing is letting go of 'Mother Church,' as you knew it from your youth. That is as difficult as letting go of one's birth family."

Joan Chittister says in her book *Scarred by Struggle, Transformed by Hope* that struggle is a gift of new life in disguise: "Struggle is, in other words, the gift of new life in disguise. A hard gift perhaps. A strong gift indeed. But a gift without which we run the risk of going to our graves only half-alive."[31]

I hope the new life I have created for myself is a sign of hope for others. Many people, particularly my therapist and my closest friends, have played a significant role in helping me to heal. I could never have done it alone and without professional help. At the end of the day, I have to acknowledge that my abuser was a catalyst that led me to a much deeper exploration of who I am. The experience of abuse by a Catholic priest led me down a path of self-knowledge, healing, and recovery. I wouldn't wish the abuse on anyone in order to gain that type of self-knowledge, but it was the journey I experienced. As Richard Rohr says so succinctly, "everything belongs."[32]

Ψ COMMENTARY

Our empathy instantly goes to the victim in this story. It is difficult to comprehend the cruelty this priest perpetrated on her. That a priest would groom, manipulate, and emotionally abuse a vulnerable young girl for many years,

166

eventually using her for his sexual compulsions, is horrific and inordinately contrary to our understanding of who a religious leader is called to be.

It is very hard to have any compassion for this priest. His behavior certainly deserves our full condemnation. And then I wonder. What is his story? What is the story behind this story? What possibly could have happened to this gifted priest to cause him to descend into such cruelly abusive behavior? As we have seen from the previous stories of abusive priests, there is always a story behind the story we know about them. Was this man himself a victim of abuse or some other significant trauma? Was he in the grips of some mental illness or addiction? What would we feel if we knew the story? Without his story we feel only anger, or even rage at his inhumane treatment of this victim. If we knew his story, would that allow us also to feel some compassion for him as well?

An Angry Abuser

We do know this priest represents a type of abuser for whom the abuse is not only about a sickened sexuality, but also about anger, control, and abuse of power. All abuse involves an abuse of power. An individual with more power, whether priest, father, mother, uncle, older sibling, etc., uses that power to impose his or her will or sickness on the less powerful, the young, the vulnerable, the trusting. The abusive coercion of power and the consequent betrayal of trust are as damaging as the sexual harm inflicted. It leads the victim to great anxiety, a loss of a sense of safety, and difficulty ever trusting again, sometimes for life.

Priests and other religious leaders have great power because of the special role and trust with which we endow them. As it has been said, absolute power corrupts absolutely, even with a priest. This priest is especially egregious in his use of his priestly power. He is a charismatic and also clearly a very angry man. Many years before he turned the relationship sexual, he used his power to mold and shape this woman into a virtual slave. She was taught early to obey him, no matter what she felt. She also feared his anger and his penchant for public humiliation. Long before he pushed sex on her, he had taken control over her mind and spirit. In his sickness, this priest was clearly addicted to the power that he had over his victim.

All abusers act out their sickness with those who are vulnerable to them. This is especially true of the angry, coercive, violent offender (in contrast to the more seductive abusers found in our previous stories). The victim ceases to be his or her own person and becomes just an object for the abuser to use. This is clearly seen here when the priest coerces the relationship into a sexual one. There is no mutuality in these sexual encounters. It is rape, as the therapist says. This objectifying does great damage to the victim's sense of self and personhood.

The other important characteristic of this type of abuser is that they blame the victim, something most abusers do in some way, but it is especially strong in this coercive type. It is a sadly classic moment when this victim confronts the priest about the sexual part of the abuse and he responds, "I thought I was helping you, I thought you needed it." What an incredible distortion and transfer of responsibility, especially coming from a priest! Yet this is what the abuser often believes in his delusional rational-izations, that it is not his fault. Somehow, it is the victim's fault. The victim absorbs the blame and believes the lie. This further disempowered this victim and filled her with disabling shame.

Given this priest's charismatic, angrily controlling, and manipulative power, backed by his spiritual and emotional role, it is no surprise that she became a victim of his sexual abuse. The dynamics involved, although she was eighteen at the time the abuse became sexual, were the same as when a child is abused. The victim is stripped of the personal power to say no to the abuse. In fact, this victim's abuse began when she was a child and the priest used her woundedness to intimidate and entice her into an emotionally abusive relationship. By the time she was eighteen and he coerced her into sex, she was already fully under his control.

Shaken Spirituality

This woman suffered the usual effects of abuse: her sense of powerlessness; her loss of her sense of self; her debilitating shame about the sexual relationship; her de-pression and extreme anxiety; the awful stress of keeping a shame-filled secret; her inability to stop the abuse until she got outside help; and, especially poignant, her deep woundedness and her inability to enter into relationships with men and have a married life and children like her peers. However, perhaps the most prominent wound in this story is the damage caused to her faith life, spir-ituality, and relationship to the Church. This spiritually destructive effect of clerical abuse, along with the deeper betrayal involved, makes it more damaging than abuse by most other types of perpetrators.

Because religious leaders, especially Catholic priests, are seen as representing God, a victim's spirituality and relationship to God and the Church is profoundly shaken. Internal images of God are distorted. God can be seen as abusive, betraying, abandoning, absent. The always difficult question of suffering becomes predominant and agonizing. How could God allow a priest to abuse me? Why didn't God protect me? Did God abuse or punish me, because I am bad? If a priest could abuse me, I must be especially bad! A safe harbor of faith and devotion to the Church has been made a place of danger, shame, and alienation. Although the author of this story continued to participate externally in the Church, she described an inner spiritual poverty resulting from the abuse that left her empty and hopeless.

Recovery from the spiritual effects of clerical sexual abuse is one of the most difficult parts of recovery for many survivors. Mercifully, in this story we see a journey of emotional and spiritual healing, one that is possible for all survivors. The first step was breaking the silence, shedding the immense burden of secrecy, and telling some trusted person the story of the abuse. Here the trusted person is a psychotherapist. Even with her help, there was an intense emotional struggle to speak out about the abuse. We see great shame and fear initially blocking her from finding her voice and breaking the silence.

We also see the immense relief and self-empowerment that began to develop after she shared the secret and her therapist listened and validated her story and her pain.

The therapist offered her critical words, vital for healing: "This is not your fault." Such empathy and validation is critical to a victim's healing. This is why the Church's past response of attempting to keep the abuse secret, requiring the victim to sign a gag order as part of a settlement, was so damaging. What a contrast to the response of Mother Teresa of Calcutta, who believed this victim's story, validated her, and then helped her to put the abuse in the context of healing spiritual meaning.

Empowered by revealing her secret to her therapist, this victim found the strength to stop the abuse and stand up to her abuser. This was met by violent resistance, including an attempted rape by the priest, which dramatically demonstrates how difficult it is for a victim to stop abuse on her own. Imagine a child trying to stand up to the abuser and stop the abuse! The power of the abuser over the victim is just too strong, particularly if the abuser is a priest.

A part of this healing step is to move beyond the safety of the therapist's office and break the silence in some more public way. This victim first told a small circle of family and friends of the abuse. She was listened to, validated, and supported. This empowered her to tell Church authorities and break the silence completely. Here she met a very mixed response.

This victim's experience with the Church's hierarchy has been all too common for other victims, at least in the past. The victims' needs to be heard, validated, treated compassionately, and pastorally reassured all too often have not been understood or have been ignored. If the Church had responded with compassion, openness, and decisive action toward the abusers, they would have aided in the gospel ministry of healing for victims, as well as avoiding much of the legal and financial devastation of recent years.

The next step in this victim's healing was getting in touch with her anger. This is a vital phase of the healing process. Feeling and expressing her anger at the abuse and the abuser freed her from the shame and belief that the abuse was her fault. She put responsibility where it belonged, on her abuser. This liberates the victim from his or her position of helplessness and fear. The victim experiences the personal power taken away by the abuser start to return. This comes from directing the anger where it belongs. It is important to emphasize, however, that this is a temporary stage. Some victims become stuck at this level. They can become bitter in their anger or even use their anger to victimize or abuse others. They remain victims, now angry victims, if they do not move beyond their justifiable anger.

In this story, the victim moved to another step of healing, beyond her anger, by facing and grieving her losses caused by the abuse. She mourned the loss of innocence and the loss of time, especially the crucial time of her young adulthood. She mourned the loss of healthy relationships with men, and the loss of marriage and children. She grieved the loss of her original faith and spirituality. Chronic, stuck anger often hides this necessary pain of grieving. Her courage to grieve freed her to take charge of her life on her terms, really for the first time. She does this most powerfully in her spiritual journey of healing her soul and recovering and recreating her faith and relationship with God and the Church.

Core Healing

The healing journey for victims is not then just about psychological healing; it is also about spiritual healing and growth. This is especially true for victims of clerical abuse, yet is true for all other victims of abuse as well. It involves three core spiritual processes that are essential to healing: forgiveness, discovery of meaning and purpose for the suffering, and transforming the abuse experience into some kind of service for others. We see all three aspects of healing in this story.

Forgiveness, not a one-time act or choice but an ongoing process, at some point needs to become a part of the healing process. This does not mean excusing the abuse; rather it includes letting go of the anger at the abuser, praying for the abuser, and eventually seeing the wounded, shared humanity underneath his abusive behavior. This is very difficult, long-term, yet necessary psycho-spiritual work.

The victim will not be able to move on into a new, freer chapter in his or her life until this is done. Paradoxically, if stuck in anger, the victim continues to be controlled by the abuser, now through his or her own anger.

Our clinical experience has demonstrated to us that an important part of recovery from trauma and tragedy is the ability to place this destructive experience into a context of spiritual meaning. All three victims whose stories are told in this book found great comfort and solace in discovering meaning and even purpose in the suffering caused by their abuse by a priest. The search for this meaning was often long and arduous. Finding meaning in such a destructive act as childhood or adolescent sexual abuse is quite daunting. Yet each of these survivors of abuse found meaning from various spiritual resources. This proved to be vital in their healing process and enabled them to transcend and then even transform their suffering into new purpose for their lives. Viktor Frankl, a Jewish psychiatrist who survived the Holocaust at Auschwitz, states in his landmark book *Man's Search for Meaning* that those who best survived the unspeakable horrors of the concentration camps were those who were able to find meaning in their suffering.[33] Patrick Carnes, the pioneer clinician, researcher, and teacher in the area of sexual addiction, writes, "I believe survivors of any form of abuse have that essential task. Out of the indescribable pain comes clarity of belief and depth of purpose."[34]

The victim in this story found consolation and healing meaning in the words that Mother Teresa spoke to her: "We must trust and have confidence that Jesus walks with us through everything, that our suffering was his suffering first. When we are suffering so much, it is Jesus that is kissing us....He knows it is the way to holiness." She understood that God loves us through the suffering, using it to bring us spiritual growth and maturity, even if that suffering is unjust.

The final spiritual movement for this victim involves capturing the meaning and purpose in the abuse experience and transforming it into service of others. She developed a deep compassion and empathy with the poor, with service to AIDS victims, with anyone who is oppressed or abused in any way. Instead of being stuck in helplessness and bitterness, she allowed her abuse experience to lead to deeper faith and spiritual empowerment. She saw her inner poverty of spirit and embraced its connection to the dire physical poverty of the poor in India, in Los Angeles, and elsewhere. Her service to the poor moved her out of herself and her pain to a larger perspective and life. She used the pain of her abuse experience as a gift that led to deep compassion for others who suffer.

A key part of this victim's spiritual healing involved her encounters with people of deep faith who believed in her and supported her. The deep spirituality of her therapist, the profound wisdom, compassion, and faith of Mother Teresa of Calcutta, the faith of her "soul friends," all help to witness to her that faith, hope, and love are still possible in the face of abuse. Every victim of clergy abuse needs such mentors of spirit to revive their soul and rebuild their faith.

At the end of her journey, this victim achieved a level of spiritual healing, maturity, forgiveness, and serenity that any of us could aspire to. She saw that her struggle to heal from the abuse in some ways became a blessing. She even acknowledged that her abuser was a catalyst, leading to a deeper knowing of herself. Nothing can justify or minimize the wrongness or damage of the abuse. Yet she expressed the truth that God can use anything in our lives, even the horror of abuse, to lead us to a deeper relationship with ourselves, with our deepest spiritual selves, and with the God of our understanding. This courageous victim, although scarred, lives a new life of freedom, purpose, service, spirit, and hope, truly a spirit resurrected.

Eight

A SURVIVOR
WHO WANTED TO PLEASE

My story begins when I was born in the 1950s into a Catholic family of seven children. I was the youngest. I start there because I have come to believe that I have always been an approval seeker. My father was an alcoholic, and I guess I always sought his approval and acknowledgment that I was acceptable. Religion was a big part of my family life, and I learned at an early age that, if I could live a religious life, then people would respect me, even my parents.

So while I was in seventh grade, I started to look into the seminary. The first place I went for guidance was my parish priest, the assistant pastor, who had taken a liking to me. When I became an altar boy one of the perks was doing the funerals and weddings in the parish. The funerals took me out of school, and I was paid for the weddings. When I mentioned to this priest my interest in the seminary, my selections for the funerals and weddings increased tenfold. Another perk for me was that the priest always left an ample amount of wine after the Mass and told me it was all right if I drank it all before taking the goblets back to the rectory. So I would get a little buzz before I went back to my classes after a funeral, or a good feeling after a wedding. In my mind it was the start of a friendship.

SWIMMING ALONE

One day when I was in eighth grade, this priest had borrowed a convertible for the parish picnic. He invited me to ride with him in the parade. After going to the amusement park, he asked me if I would like to go with him to return the car to its owners. I asked my mother, and she said it would be fine as my parents were also friends with the people who had lent him the car. The people had a beautiful home in a nice neighborhood with a built-in heated swimming pool. When we arrived at their house no one was home. The priest explained to me that they were gone on vacation. He showed me through their home and took me into the basement to show me that they had a keg of beer in the refrigerator, with a tap outside by the pool.

We went outside, he gave me a beer mug and we started to drink some beer. He asked if I wanted to go for a swim. There was a fog coming off the pool as the water was heated. I explained to him that I did not have a swimming suit. He stated that it was all right, we could skinny dip and no one would see us because the pool was surrounded by trees and the fog was coming off the pool. I told him I was not comfortable with that, and he went inside and got a pair of swimming trunks for me.

After having quite a few beers, I put on the swimming trunks, which were a little too large for me. I jumped into the pool and started to swim around. The next thing I knew, the priest was in his underpants and jumping into the pool. He swam over to me in the deep end and took my swimming trunks off me. I was stunned. I got out of the pool, went inside the house, dried off, and put on my clothes. I was feeling the effects of the beer and was just stunned. The priest came in, dried himself off in front of me, got dressed, and then said, "Let's have another beer." We did, and then he took me home. On the way home he caressed me and told me he was sorry if I had felt uncomfortable. He was trying to reassure me that everything was okay and probably hoping I would not tell my parents. I already knew in my mind that I could not tell anyone. However, the number of funerals and weddings I served for increased.

During that school year, seminarians came to our school and gave a presentation about seminary life. They invited us out to the seminary. After visiting the seminary one Friday night, I met some other guys who were visiting from another parish. We got along pretty well and the seminarian who had brought them told us we could go to the seminary any Friday night we wanted to. He would pick up the guys from his parish and then come to my house to get me. We would stop and get some Cold Duck to drink and then go to the seminary to listen to music and shoot pool. This was okay with my parents because I was with a seminarian.

That summer we went to the seminary for the altar boys' picnic. The seminary had an outdoor pool and great grounds for a barbecue and picnic. The priest from my parish took us. We played in the pool and played a game of water polo. The priest and I were on opposing teams. He always marked me, and often grabbed me. I knew in my mind that something was wrong with this. However, I discounted it as being just part of the game. When I was in the dressing room changing, he came into the room and watched me. Again, it felt strange. Then he singled me out to come with him and served me some beer. Now I felt special, treated better than the rest of my classmates.

I took and passed the entrance exam to the high school seminary. The summer before high school began, I got together quite often with the seminarian who had taken us to the Friday night parties, and with the young guys from the other parishes. We all played soccer together, and I was excited to get started with school. During the first year of the seminary, the seminarian would take us out occasionally, and we would always get some beer or wine to drink. Also during my freshman year, I got to know another priest, one of my teachers. My parish priest and the teacher knew each other.

At Christmas break the seminarians went to their parishes to help with Christmas Masses. At Easter break, we did the same thing. Our parish priests took us to dinner during the break. The night of the dinner, my parish priest picked me up, along with another seminarian, to take us to the dinner. Once there, the priest said it was okay for us to order a drink. I had a whiskey sour cocktail. Actually I had a couple. The priest sat next to me and ordered more drinks and let me have his. At the end of the evening, we drove the other seminarian home, and then the priest asked if I wanted to spend the night at the rectory. He called my parents and told them that I was going to spend the night there. He told them that all the seminarians were there and he would bring me home in the morning. I had had way too much to drink. I remember going to the rectory and the priest telling me to be extra quiet as we walked past the pastor's room. We went into his room, and he turned on some music and made some more drinks.

The next thing I remember, I was naked and the priest was holding my penis with one hand and holding himself

179

with his other hand. Ignorant about sex, I didn't know what he was doing. I now know that he was jerking himself off while doing me at the same time. I was so scared. I waited until he passed out and then called one of my friends from the seminary who could drive. He came to the rectory and picked me up. It was very early in the morning and he had snuck out of his house to come get me. I spent the night in his basement. After throwing up several times, and getting a little sleep, I walked home. His house was far from mine, but when I got home my dad was up, and I told him I had walked home from the rectory.

I only saw this priest again when I went to church or served Mass. Ironically, he conducted the marriage celebration for one of my sisters. That was an awkward day. I think he knew that I did not tell anyone about what happened.

During my sophomore year at the seminary, the older seminarian I spoke of earlier frequently hung around high school. He often asked me to go out with him for drinks. One night he called my parents and told them some seminarians were spending the night at the advanced seminary. Though this was not allowed, he took us out to dinner, bought us some wine, and snuck us into the advanced seminary. We drank and spent the night in the seminary tower. That Christmas he offered me a job with his family's business delivering flowers. We delivered flowers every day the weekend before Christmas. I made some money and felt in debt to him. One weekend, he had me spend the night at the seminary. However, he told me I could not tell anyone. We stayed in his room. I remember him asking me to get undressed, and I told him, no, I would sleep with my clothes on. We both slept in his bed. He rubbed my back all night.

On another occasion, he invited me and a fellow class-mate to spend the night at his parents' house. He took us out drinking, and then we went back to his home. He had the two of us get undressed in front of him. I truly do not recall what else happened that night. However, later in the week, when my classmate and I were in study hall together, we discussed that evening. He told me that we should tell someone at the seminary what happened. I was afraid that if I did, I would be kicked out of the seminary. I felt I could not do that because my dad had lost his job and I would have nowhere to go. I kept silent.

During my junior year, I had a class with the same teacher I had gotten to know in my freshman year. He lived in an apart-ment by himself. He took me to the racetrack occasionally to watch the horses. My parents were okay with this. As time went on, he also took me over to his apartment. I confided to him all that had happened to me. I was going through a depression. I had tried to commit suicide a couple of times. He took me to see a doctor he knew, who prescribed some medicine for me. On my birthday, he had a surprise party for me at his apartment. A couple of other seminarians were there, and my mom and dad even came by. After that, my stays at the apartment were more frequent. My parents were not concerned about it. He bought me beer and had me take Jacuzzi baths and then rubbed me down with an alcohol rub. One time, I passed out and then woke up naked in his bed with him sleeping next to me. I had a sticky substance on my body. I had no idea what it was at that time. Now I know it was his semen.

My senior year at the seminary was very difficult for me. I was desperately depressed. I tried to commit suicide again. I met another priest at the seminary and mustered the courage to tell him everything that had happened to me. He explained to me that you could not be friends with older people or priests. I took his advice and had no further contact with anyone at the seminary. I graduated from the seminary and stopped going to church all together.

FORGIVING THOSE WHO TRESPASSED

As I look back upon those events, I am still ashamed and feel guilt about what happened. It seems altogether too much to comprehend. How many times did I look for acceptance from a priest or seminarian, only to be abused? I had wanted to be a priest so others would look up to me; here I was being abused by priests. I feel at times that the abuse was my fault, that I didn't do enough to stop it, that I was a failure.

These abuse events led to me having a very difficult time with relationships. I had sex with a woman for the first time when I was in college. This was a very traumatic experience for me. However, she was six years older than me and had experience. She taught me about sex and then fell in love with me, two things I knew nothing about. The sex was great, but I did not understand love. She got pregnant and wanted to get married. Again I was full of guilt and shame. I told her I could not marry her. She had a miscarriage and moved out of state. I continued to have a very difficult time dating women. When I finally met someone else, we did not have sex; we just dated each other for two years, then married. I was the first man she had ever been with. We now have been married for twenty-five years and have three beautiful children.

While the events in my youth caused me to have a difficult time with relationships, I have also had difficulty with drinking and with my religion. In addition, it has always been hard for me to be totally honest with others and with myself. You see, I have kept a big secret inside myself for a very long time.

My healing began when I admitted that I was an alcoholic. I entered a Twelve-Step program and got a sponsor. In step four we make a list of all those persons we have harmed. This is when the abuse started to come up again in my life. My sponsor suggested that I go into therapy. It was during this therapy process that I shared what had happened to me. About that time I saw the movie *Good Will Hunting*. There is a part in this movie where the therapist learns of his patient's past. He tells the patient that the past hurtful events were not his fault. He continues telling the patient this until the patient can believe it himself. That is what happened to me. I knew at that point that the abuse was not my fault. I started the process of forgiving myself.

Because of the AA program, I have learned many liberating things, and now I am on a new journey of life. I have experienced a spiritual awakening. Once I faced the demons of my past, I began to forgive myself, and with that I could forgive others. I made a choice not to shut the door on the past, and it opened a door to a brighter future. I reconciled myself to God. I always felt that God protected me; I just did not understand what had happened to me, why he allowed these terrible things to happen to me. I know today he allowed these things to happen so I might learn how to help others. I believe that God's plan is working. Today I use all my experiences to try to help others. I believe that the reason for everyone's existence is to help others as Jesus Christ helped all of us.

It may seem ironic that I originally went to the seminary with the belief that I should give my life to God by becoming a priest and now I give over my life to God as a result of the AA program. I share my experience, strength, and hope with others so that I, and hopefully others, can have a living relationship with God. I may not ever totally understand in this human existence why things happened the way they did. However, today I have a conscious contact with my God, and I turn everything over to God. I know that the only way I can forgive myself is to forgive those who trespassed against me. I don't have to understand it or seek revenge for it. I can forgive, as I believe God has forgiven me.

Ψ COMMENTARY

In the clipped, spare simplicity of this story we hear the powerful tale of a young boy's search for approval from priests, approval that his father had failed to give, and instead finding multiple abuse. We follow his journey from the near-fatal effects of this abuse to his current healing, serenity, and forgiveness.

He is sexually abused by three men whom he turned to for spiritual guidance and acceptance, men he looked to as father figures: his parish priest, an older seminarian, and a priest teacher at his high school seminary. Each of them takes advantage of his youthfulness and emotional vulnerability and need. All victims are vulnerable in some way. Their childhood lack of knowledge, especially about sex, their lack of personal power, and their innate desire to trust and be special to an admired adult makes them vulnerable. Deeper emotional vulnerability such as this boy's need for a father to replace his alcoholic, emotionally unavailable father makes the child even more susceptible to abuse.

In their sickness all three perpetrators use this boy's neediness mercilessly. This boy wanted simply to be seen as worthwhile and perhaps become a priest like them. Victims of abuse are not seeking sex; rather they may be hoping unconsciously that some emotional need will be met. Instead, his religious abusers plied him with alcohol, enticed him with special treatment, and led him into very exploitative, unwanted sexual encounters. The final abuse by his priest teacher, to whom he confided his depression, suicide attempts, and previous abuse, is especially reprehensible. The young man trustingly goes to him for comfort, healing, and guidance. What he gets is more abuse. His trust is betrayed again. Later in depression and despair, he attempts suicide once more. Mercifully, he finally finds a priest he can trust who provides some comfort and the sadly necessary advice that "you could not be friends with older people or priests." One wonders what this apparently healthy priest did with the information about the abusing priests.

An Imbalance of Power

This story raises a frequently asked question (often by the victims themselves): why can't a young person just say no and stop the abuse? We wonder particularly, as in this story, when there are multiple, sequential abusers and the victim is older, an adolescent. This story illustrates the answer. The difference in physical and psychological power is paramount. There is also the vulnerability and neediness of the child and the consequent deep desire to trust. In addition, each experience of abuse renders the young person ever more helpless, paralyzed by fear and shame. All of this strips the young person of the ability to say no or stop the abuse without outside help. The child or even adolescent becomes more vulnerable to the next abuser who may appear.

We see clearly in this story the far-reaching and long-lasting damage caused by the trauma of sexual abuse, especially if perpetrated by clergy. Because of the abuse, and possibly also because of his dysfunctional family dynamics, this man suffered from serious and dangerous depression during his adolescence. Having attempted suicide several times, he is lucky to be alive today. The abuse also appears to have contributed to his later development of alcoholism. His priest abusers introduced him to drinking and used it as a part of the abuse. Certainly his father's alcoholism genetically predisposed him to alcoholism as well. Substance abuse or addiction is a frequent consequence of childhood sexual abuse.

We see again the high levels of shame and very low self-esteem caused by the abuse. He is flooded with false guilt, feeling that the abuse was his fault, feeling that he should have been able to stop it or tell someone. Victims are so full of shame and erroneous self-blame they are terrified to tell anyone. They hold their secret deep within, frightened that someone will find out and condemn them. This led to the author's difficulty being honest with others and even with himself. Fearful of what is remembered within, fearful of what others would think of him if they knew his secret, he lives in dread of being open or close to others.

This obviously caused difficulty in his relationships. The author describes his painful experience in relationships with women, his difficulty trusting, being open, getting close, and being sexually intimate. Many victims have a great struggle with trust in relationships and with the sexual dimension of relationships. Since the betrayal of trust is especially deep in clergy abuse, the damage to the victim's ability to trust in relationships may be even greater. The developing sexuality of the young person is particularly wounded in clerical abuse. Every victim of sexual abuse experiences some damage to their sexuality: fear, anxiety, shame, flashbacks, and sometimes lasting sexual dysfunction. Male victims of male perpetrators suffer considerable sexual identity confusion and shame. Sexual abuse by a priest heightens all of this. The confusion is greater, the shame is deeper. The victim feels that if I "caused" a holy celibate priest to be sexual with me, I, and my sexual feelings, must be really bad; God will punish me severely for my sexuality.

The spiritual damage following clerical abuse is profound in this story as well. The young man who wanted to be a priest left the seminary and stopped going to church altogether. The loss of what he felt to be a true calling is still troubling to him, even though he is happy with his present family life. His image of God and consequently his relationship with God became distorted, distrusting, and painful. He wondered why God did not protect him. He believed for a time that God allowed him to be abused by priests in order to hurt him. God becomes for this victim a punishing, vengeful abuser, not to be trusted or allowed close, an image of God created by representatives of God.

Hope and eventually faith returned for him, not because of any Church figure, but through AA's spiritual recovery principles and through spiritually sensitive psychotherapy.[35] Through AA he was first enabled to surrender his destructive, compulsive drinking. In his sobriety he learned to be honest with himself and with others in the program. His therapist helped him to see that the abuse was not his fault. This empowered him to forgive himself. His shame and self-loathing decreased, eventually largely disappearing.

He experienced a spiritual awakening, and felt reconciled to God. He developed a new image of God, a God not out to hurt him. He found that God helped him use the abuse he suffered to teach him how to help others. This is God's plan for him. This man uses his life experience, including the clerical abuse, to be of service to others in and out of the AA recovery community. Although the abuse nearly led him to take his life, he now leads a deeply satisfying life seeking to follow the call he now hears from God.

Reclaiming Power

An especially powerful part of his healing and spiritual awakening was his ability to forgive the priests and the seminarian who abused him. Forgiving himself, feeling forgiven by God, led him to forgive his abusers. He let go of anger and any desire for revenge.

In recent years there has been much study of the power and importance of forgiveness even in secular psychological literature.[36] For the victim, forgiveness might at first feel impossible or even offensive. It might appear to be condoning the abuse. It might also feel frightening to let go of the rightful sense of power that healing anger finally restores to the victim. It might seem to the victims that forgiveness puts them back into the helpless, powerless victim role. However, forgiveness actually empowers the victims, giving them an opportunity to move past their anger and reclaim their wholeness and innocence. Forgiveness releases them from their last ties to any remaining power the abuse and the abuser have over them.

Another important part of the spiritual power of such forgiveness is that it enables victims to see the shared humanity of themselves and their offenders. A victim has been used as a sexual object by the abuser and so has experienced being dehumanized and depersonalized, something abuse does to both the victim and the abuser. Part of healing for the victim is to rediscover the beauty and dignity of his or her personhood and humanity. To do this fully, the victim is also challenged to see the core humanity of the abuser as well. Forgiveness empowers a victim to see the wounded, sinful, yet glorious, human journey shared with the offender. Without forgiveness, we diminish our humanity and block our healing journey.

A priest in leadership in his diocese once said that the victims of abuse do not care whether the priests get help; they just want them locked up in prison. This is generally not my experience with victims. Some victims want to punish their abusers. Most want first and foremost for their

189

abusers to be removed from any situation in which they can harm any more young people. Many victims are heartened to know that the priest is getting treatment, with hope that he might recover from his sickness. Forgiveness is a mutual desire for healing and peace. Forgiveness forced before its time is empty and even damaging to the healing process. Forgiveness never chosen, however, is corrosive of the soul and blocks the path of healing.

Nine

A SURVIVOR
WHO SAID NOT A WORD

〜〜〜〜〜

When I was a little girl, four years old, my family — consisting of my mother, father, and two older brothers, aged five and eight, and younger sister, just six months — lived together in a tiny three-bedroom house across an alley from our parish church. As you left the side door of our house, you immediately stepped into this alley, which also served as the driveway for our three priests to get to their rectory. Our pastor, Monsignor, was alcoholic. He sometimes caused us quite a scare. He would come driving his car madly down the alley at a high rate of speed, wildly honking, sending us terrified children scrambling back onto the stoop as he whipped by. In one incident, Monsignor ran over and crushed my brothers' tricycle and bicycle.

Since we rented this house from the church, Monsignor was our landlord and had a key to the house. One day my mother, an attractive young woman in her early thirties, was doing the laundry downstairs in the basement. I was upstairs, and my baby sister was asleep. No one else was at home. Monsignor used his key to enter the house, went downstairs into the dark basement, and in a drunken rage sexually assaulted my mother. Hearing her scream, I rushed downstairs and saw what he was doing to my mother. Then the priest attacked and molested me. Then Monsignor left.

My mother yelled hysterically at me to go up upstairs and leave her alone. Being obedient, I went upstairs, my rectum hurting from Monsignor's finger puncturing it. Later my mother came upstairs, and we folded laundry together and then ate ice cream. The sweetness of the ice cream eased the pain and the work kept my mind off the craziness I felt inside. My mother did not say a word about what had occurred in the basement. It was never talked about at all. When the lease was up, we moved away from that house. No charges were filed. No one was told. Nothing was ever said. We simply left.

NOT A DREAM

This memory first came to me in a dream, which in a few days crystallized into a clear memory. I was around fifty when this occurred. I had become a psychotherapist and had been working for several years with female survivors of verbal, emotional, physical, and sexual abuse. Some of these women had been abused by priests. Listening to their stories in therapy brought forth the long-buried memory of my own abuse experience. I felt great pain when the memory surfaced, yet I also felt more sane and balanced. The memory of my mother's molestation and my abuse was a key piece of the puzzle of my life that I had been missing. Now certain mysteries about my family and myself finally made sense.

The day after my dream, I called my oldest brother and recounted it to him. I asked him to describe what he remembered of that house. With his help I was able to draw the floor plan and the basement. What I remembered fit the layout of the house. Also, certain events in my life that had always puzzled me began to fall into place. I had always vividly remembered an experience in a doctor's office when I was about four or five; this occurred, I realize now, after the abuse, but I had never understood my reaction to the experience. I was sick and had been brought to the pediatrician's office. The whole family was with me in the exam room. I was lying face down on the exam table, fully clothed except for my winter snow leggings, which were pulled down with my little bottom exposed. The pediatrician inserted a rectal thermometer, an ordinary procedure with a young child, but my reaction was extreme. I froze with terror and shame. I wanted to hide, yet could not move a muscle. I wanted to scream, but could not utter any words or make any sound. Until I recalled the abuse, I never understood why this experience in the doctor's office had been so awful for me. I know now that the rectal thermometer triggered emotions and body memories from my abuse by the Monsignor.

The memory of the abuse also helped me comprehend my mother's erratic behavior when I was growing up. She had many outbursts of hysteria and extreme anxiety and suffered frequent migraines. Minor events would trigger her unpredictably. I remember my mother walking me to school one rainy day. Cars driving by splashed some water on us. My mother went into a fit of out-of-control hysteria right there on the street. I was frightened and embarrassed, not knowing what to do to get my mother back in control. From four years of age on, I became my mother's guardian, caretaker, and chief assistant. I helped take care of her for my father when she was distraught.

It is difficult for me to entirely tease out what problems the abuse caused me, and what came from difficulties in my family. I am sure that they interacted, both for me and for my family. I think that my mother's abuse had a significant impact on her emotional stability, on her parenting, and on my parents' marriage. This tension in their relationship affected my siblings and me. I was aware of some of their difficulties as I was growing up, but I never understood what caused them. They eventually divorced when I was in my forties.

As a child, I bit my fingernails until they bled and tore at my toenails until they did the same. I wet the bed until I was quite old, which I was very ashamed of. Late in developing breasts and menstruating, I was flat chested and didn't wear a bra like the other girls my age. This added to the shame I already felt, especially about my body. I am aware now that I may have unconsciously avoided some of my developing sexual feelings. I was less aware of and less interested in sex than most of my peers. I imagine that this was a direct effect of the abuse. My self-esteem was very low. I felt isolated and alone, and at times I just wanted to hide. To this day, I struggle with a tendency to numb my emotions by compulsively eating sweets or carbohydrates, as my mother and I did that day after the abuse.

Ironically, one of my salvations was boys. I became best friends with a neighbor boy when I was five. We did everything together. We were like sister and brother and remained close friends until he died quite suddenly when we were thirty. I was a tomboy and loved to play football and other rough sports with him and my brothers. All of this helped me to feel better about myself. If I could be one of the boys, for that time, I felt worthwhile and all right about myself.

194

As I got older and went to junior high school, I began to look up to certain girls as models or mentors. One was a drummer in the school band; I became a percussionist in the band. Another was a cheerleader. I so much wanted to be a cheerleader, but my low self-esteem kept me from thinking that I could be one. Nonetheless, I tried out. Afterward I ran to church and prayed before the statue of the Blessed Mother. Was there any way? Miraculously, I was one of only two sophomores chosen for the cheerleading squad. I could not believe it! This did wonders for my flagging self-confidence. Still, until my forties, I often was unable to speak up for myself when I was treated unfairly. I sometimes felt like an object to be used or manipulated for someone else's purposes with no voice to protest or assert my own feelings or needs. I was an outgoing, bubbly, Pollyanna cheerleader on the outside, but inside I was often locked up and frozen.

POTENTIAL FOR LOVE

A major transformation came when I studied with Virginia Satir, a pioneer in the development of family therapy and the human potential movement. She became my teacher, mentor, and friend. In her experiential training, she taught me to find and trust my inner voice. She helped me to embrace and love myself with a new sense of my own personal worth and power. Through her, I learned to speak up about what was abusive or no longer fit for me in my life. My healing from the abuse began in my work with Satir even though I did not yet remember the abuse.

Working as a therapist with women who had been emotionally, verbally, physically, or sexually abused was healing and liberating for me as well. As much as they healed in our work together, I was healed in return, both before and after the memory of my abuse surfaced. Helping them find their voice, break the silence, and speak the truth of what had been done to them; helping them overcome their debilitating shame and free themselves from their paralyzing fear; helping them become the women God had created them to be; all this reflected and invigorated the process that I was undergoing at the same time.

After remembering my abuse, I had periods of anger at Monsignor. It was healing for me for a short time to imagine chopping him up into bits, chopping off his penis, chopping off his fingers. I knew this was simply an antidote to my shame and to my childhood helplessness. I meant him no harm and usually bear no anger for him now, although periodically anger whooshes up from deep within me, especially about how his actions affected my mother and through her my whole family. However, I wonder what his story was, what his wound might have been, that he did such an awful thing. The main anger I sometimes feel now is not at priest perpetrators of abuse, but at the hierarchy and Church leadership who have been in denial and hiding this wound in the Church. Then I remember that they most likely are wounded as well. I sometimes feel sadness for my mother that she never received any help for her pain. I wonder how life would have been different for her and my family if she had been consoled.

It is unclear to me how the abuse affected me spiritually. My earliest spiritual influences came from women: my two grandmothers, my mother, and a nun, Mother Leoline, who taught me religion in first grade. It was said of my father's mother, who had very little but was incredibly generous, that if Lucifer himself showed up at her door, she would ask

196

him to come in, put another potato in the pot, and invite him to sit down and eat at the family table. My maternal grandmother was similarly full of unconditional love. Mother Leoline impressed upon my young mind that this was the same kind of love God had for each of us. Through this simple, yet remarkable woman, early in my life I came to believe in God's unconditional love. I wanted to be like these women and love unconditionally as they did.

Despite what the Monsignor did to my mother and me, I never resented or feared priests. In fact they have been a central part of my life, partly because the other two priests at the parish where I was abused were such wonderful young priests. They brought great joy and fun into the house when they visited. They were warm, outgoing Irishmen, one quite tall, the other rather short. One became a bishop, the other a monsignor and a prominent pastor. They remained life-long friends of our family. My experiences with priests during the rest of my growing up were similarly very positive. During my nursing training, I became close to several seminarians and priests and remained friends with them. Priest friends continued to bring joy into my house when I was a married woman raising a family of my own. When I went back to work in my early forties, first into pastoral care and then into counseling, I worked with priests as colleagues, clients, and friends. A significant part of my professional career has been focused on helping in the psychospiritual training and formation of future priests in the novitiate of a Catholic religious order of men. This is work that I have deeply loved and treasured.

In the past few years I have joined my husband in doing group and individual counseling with priests and brothers who have severe psychological or addiction problems and who live in a residential recovery community. Many of them have sexually abused children or adolescents. Many of them are victims of abuse just like me. I am a survivor of abuse by a priest and am a therapist who has worked extensively with women who have been abused, and now I am a therapist to priests and brothers who have perpetrated abuse. This is an amazing turn of God's providence! What is most amazing to me is how much I love these men. I was afraid I might hate them. I do hate what they did to their victims. I hate the sickness and addiction that led them to abuse. Sometimes I feel guilty that I love them. As a survivor of abuse and after working with so many victims of abuse, I sometimes think I should not love them. Yet I do.

I love them especially when I see the shining light of their spirit, and even holiness, emerge in their core goodness: When I see them striving for recovery and healing from their emotional sickness and addiction. When I see their tears and hear their sorrow, remorse, and deep pain for their victims and for the damage they now realize they have done to their victims and to the Church they love. When I hear of their daily prayer for their victims' healing. When I see them, often for the first time, loving themselves, loving each other, and forming community among themselves. When I see them overcoming their deep shame, finally accepting themselves, opening themselves to God's unconditional love and becoming at peace at last with themselves and their past. I love them simply because they are my brothers. Perhaps this is the last chapter in the healing of my abuse. As I work to be an instrument of healing for these wounded brothers, I am completing my healing as well.

Ψ COMMENTARY

Some readers might think that Sue Lauber-Fleming's story is too good to be true. They might say that her progress in healing and her forgiving, accepting spirit toward her abuser and toward the priest abusers she now works with sounds too positive, too hopeful, perhaps even a regression to the Pollyanna persona she displayed earlier in her life. However, anyone who knows Sue well, as I have been blessed to know her, knows that her fierce commitment to truth and integrity does not allow her to sugarcoat her experience and personal truth. Sue's healing and unconditional love even for abusers is a hard-won gift that has grown from her intense commitment to her own personal journey of healing, her intense thirst and courage for personal and professional growth, and her deep spirituality.

Not All Priests Are Alike

Although Sue's experience with the monsignor was severely traumatic, some factors may have mitigated the effects on her. Since the family was incapable of speaking about what happened, Sue had no outlet for talking about her abuse experience. Consequently, her young mind worked to protect her from the unbearable memory by repressing it into her unconscious until she was ready much later in life to handle it.

The effect of the abuse was probably also mitigated by some aspects of the abuse itself. It was a one-time experience, although a very traumatic one, rather than an ongoing experience of abuse. Second, it was for the most part nonrelational abuse. Mercifully, the monsignor had not developed a trusting relationship with her. In fact, Sue and her family already knew him to be a menace; consequently the betrayal of trust, which is one of the most damaging aspects of abuse, was minimized. In addition, Sue was blessed with very positive experiences with the two associate priests who modeled for her what priests could be like at their best. This enabled her not to generalize her abuse experience to all priests or to all men. None of this is to say that what Sue experienced with Monsignor was not terrible and damaging to her, merely that some aspects of her experience protected and helped her. Sadly, this is seldom true for victims of abuse.

Recent psychological study has focused on the amazing phenomenon of "resilient children."[37] These children, despite neglect and abuse, are able to overcome their adversities and remain relatively healthy psychologically. What creates this resiliency in the face of trauma is not fully understood. We see aspects of this resiliency in Sue's story. She forged healthy, affirming, nonsexual and nonabusive relationships with boys and then men, some of them priests. Compensating for the deep woundedness of her mother, who may have been the primary casualty of Monsignor's abuse, Sue found healthy female models in her grandmothers and her first-grade nun. Later, she found another important female model in her mentor and teacher, Virginia Satir. Work with her brought Sue considerable healing, empowerment, and transformation even before her abuse became conscious.

Perhaps most dramatic in Sue's story is the spiritual resiliency that she developed despite being abused by a priest. Her positive experiences with other priests, and

her experience and understanding of God as unconditional love through her early female spiritual guides, gave
her a spiritual perspective and strength that greatly aided
her healing before and after her memory of the abuse
surfaced. The abuse did not block or arrest her spiritual growth. As a phase of her healing, she felt intense
anger at Monsignor, and then she was able to move on to
forgiveness and compassion.

She further displayed her spiritual health by allowing her personal experience of suffering from abuse to
be transformed and channeled into positive service to
others. This is an important aspect of healing that we
have seen in all three victims' stories. In Sue's case
this is through her professional, healing psychotherapy
work with women victims of abuse. Remarkably, it has
also involved a long career of service to priests. Sue
has dedicated much of her career to the healthy formation of future priests, teaching and modeling skills and
attitudes for healthy psychospiritual and psychosexual
human functioning. Now she is working as a catalyst for
healing and recovery for priests and brothers who, in
their woundedness, have abused. Sue is eloquent in her
expression of her love for them despite what they have
done. Perhaps we are all called to let God transform our
suffering, whatever its source, into such love.

Ultimate Worth

Sue's spirituality and one of the primary motivators of
our work is captured in a quote from Virginia Satir. Satir
writes concerning her therapy work, "It was as though I
saw through to the inner core of each being, seeing the
shining light of the spirit trapped in a thick black cylinder

of limitation and self-rejection. My effort was to enable the person to see what I saw; then, together, we could turn the black cylinder into a large lighted screen and build new possibilities."[38]

Our approach to all of our clients is in the same spirit. We look beyond their psychological problems and their dysfunctional or even abusive behavior to see the inner light of their spirit, their true and deepest selves. In doing so, we are able to see the ultimate value and worth of each individual no matter what they have experienced or what they have done. We work to help each person see this in themselves, to see and embrace their inner light and ultimate value. This is vital for victim and perpetrator alike. A scriptural way to say this is that we all are created in the image and likeness of God and so are a reflection of the divine. Each of us then is a magnificent person of value, of ultimate and immutable worth.

Sue has developed a powerful tool to promote this psycho-spiritual self-acceptance and healing, which she calls the Circle of Value. It is very effective for both victims and abusers. Essentially, it is an instrument to enable people to see and accept that no matter what they may have done as a part of their sick, addictive, abusive behavior, and no matter what they may have experienced as part of being victims of abuse, nothing can take away from (or add to) their ultimate value and worth. Our value is our spiritual inheritance; it is the light that resides at the center of each of us. It is a gift to us that cannot be taken away or even given away. It abides within us whether we are aware of it or not.

This, then, is further reason for helping these priests who have abused to tell their stories. Despite what they have done and the injury they have caused to their victims, to their Church, and to society, they remain magnificent persons of value, of transcendent spiritual worth. We have seen their inner light, though it has been obscured by their sickness, and we have seen that inner light emerge and grow brighter as they have healed and recovered.

EYES TO SEE, EARS TO HEAR

Every book of stories needs a story to end it. This brief story occurred during the last phases of writing this book. On April 2, 2005, the Saturday after Easter, a bright and chilly early spring day, I took a break from writing and went for a walk. I had gone away for the weekend to focus on writing and, hopefully, to finish the book, a project that by this time had consumed much of a year and more. I was staying at a beautiful retreat center in the country-side outside St. Louis, Windridge Solitude, lovingly run by a community of Catholic sisters, the Companions in the Infinite Love. I left my writing and my hermitage and followed a path in their woods.

As I followed the winding trail through the woods, I was struck by the starkness of the still-bare tree branches and undergrowth. The ground was covered by a thick carpet of dead leaves and littered with fallen broken branches. Different tones of gray and brown were the sole colors around me. It appeared that winter still had its grip on this forest.

The trail wound around, up and down, through this nearly depressing landscape till it brought me to a sunlit spot where small bunches of tiny, white and light purple wildflowers were peeking out of the brown mat of the forest floor. I stood there for some time admiring these first diminutive harbingers of life's return. Something flickered in the corner of my eye. I spun around and was startled to see an exquisite butterfly briefly settled upon one of the wildflowers. The first, lone butterfly of spring in this wintry woods! It flitted to the next flower, its beautiful black-and-white striped wings momentarily still and brilliant against the drab background of dead leaves, then it flew to milk another and then another flower of its nectar. I watched the butterfly, transfixed, still surprised and awed to see such beauty in a previously grim place.

Then I began to wonder. What sign was this? What meaning did these early wildflowers, this unexpected butterfly signify? My mind, of course, went to this book of stories. What hope, what terrible beauty, what transformation might be bursting forth from the ugly cocoon of the sickness and abuse we have witnessed in the priest sexual abuse scandal?

The thought that came to me was this: It will depend on whether we have eyes to see the butterfly. Ears to hear the hope in these stories. Hands to begin to write a new story. Hearts open to mending each other's broken hearts. Minds open to the unending possibilities of the human spirit. Souls receptive to the transforming love of Infinite Love, which we name God.

Patrick Fleming

Rationalization is . . . to my mind,
perhaps the leading spiritual disease
of our time. Everything conspires
with us to bury our sickest secrets
so deeply that, after a time, we are
no longer even aware that they are
there and to rationalize them so that,
eventually, we don't even realize that
they, and we, are sick. This is a
dangerous game. The health of
our souls is what is at stake here.

– Ronald Rolheiser

RESPONSIBLE
RECOVERY

Ten

CREATING A NEW STORY

There is a recently developed approach to psychology and psychotherapy called narrative therapy.[39] It proposes that the stories or narratives we tell ourselves about our personal and social realities profoundly shape our view of those realities. This narrative creates our feelings, beliefs, and choices; it even shapes and creates our personal reality itself. This is true for individuals and for social groups or communities. The great mythological stories of East and West both express and define the cultures from which they arose. An individual who views his personal narrative or life story through the prism of shame and despair will create a life that reflects such a narrative. A person who tells herself the story that she is worthless, helpless, and at the mercy of others will live her life accordingly. Someone, on the other hand, whose story is one of triumph and transcendence over great obstacles will likely experience and accomplish such victory in life. Our intent in sharing these stories is to help create a new narrative or story that victim-survivors, priest victim-abusers, Church, and society tell about the reality of the priest sexual abuse crisis.

The first narrative of the Church and society was a denial story. There was no problem or, if there was, it had to be kept hidden for the good of the Church. That failed, and the disastrous narrative damaged both victims and abusers. Victims were not heard, sometimes were blamed, their needs not ministered to. Priest abusers were not sufficiently confronted, not stopped, not given the treatment and accountability they needed. Fortunately, that narrative is now mostly, although not completely, over. Unfortunately, it has been replaced largely by a narrative of anger, punishment, adversarial relationships, fear, and limited understanding, with little compassion for the priest victim-abuser. The good news is that the problem is much more in the open where it can be dealt with. Awareness has grown and programs geared to children are being developed and implemented. Victims are finally being heard. The bad news is that there is little healing or hope in this narrative, and so the abuse cycle, as we have seen, continues.

Our hope is that a new story, gospel based, develops about the priest abuse crisis in the Church, a narrative based on truth telling, accountability, healing, compassion, forgiveness, transformation, and new life. These are the things Jesus was about in his story: healing the sick, forgiving sinners, challenging abusers (such as religious leaders who misused religion and wielded their power to oppress and abuse), giving sight to the blind, bringing hope to the despairing as he loved them all unconditionally.

The new story needs to include the truths about priest sexual abuse with no denial. The new story needs to include the victims' voices and minister to their needs. It needs also to incorporate the story of the priest abusers and their own history of being abused and victimized, allowing greater ministry to their needs as well. It needs to include a rehumanizing dialogue between victims, victim-abusers, and Church leaders. It requires accountability and forgiveness, truth, and reconciliation. Most of all, it must provide hope for healing for all parties and transformation of their common suffering into new life and purpose, what Jesus achieved in his narrative, the story of the gospel.

HEALING DIALOGUES

As mentioned before, victims and victim-abusers, priests who were also abused, share a common history of trauma. There is, consequently, a commonality of needs in their healing paths, although there are some differences as well. This commonality of needs suggests that another part of the new story can be the development of healing dialogues between victim and abuser. In the cases where we have facilitated such a dialogue, we have seen it to be profoundly moving and healing for both parties. We described one such meeting in an earlier commentary. It is vital that such meetings be facilitated by professionals with training and experience with both victims and abusers who can keep the dialogue safe and constructive. Both abuser and victim need to have achieved a certain level of recovery and healing. The abuser must have accepted full responsibility for the abuse with no rationalizations, excuses, or external blaming. Such a dialogue must start with the abuser apologizing for the abuse and owning full responsibility for the abuse and the great harm that it caused the victim.

The victim needs to have achieved sufficient healing to be able to feel safe in the presence of the abuser. Victims may also need an advocate of some kind present to support them and help them feel safe. The victim needs to feel free to express his or her emotions about the abuse, including any pain and anger, and yet be able to do so constructively. Hopefully, the victim will be ready to receive the abuser's apology. If the victim is ready to express forgiveness to the abuser, that could occur here. If not, there could be another meeting in the future.

The Church could sponsor and organize such healing dialogues between priest victim-abuser and victim. These dialogues could be part of a Church-sponsored program of what is called restorative justice. This approach attempts to avoid the adversarial relationships of civil suits. These suits may bring some victims significant monetary compensation, and tort lawyers sizable fees, but they are certainly not designed for healing for victims. They, in fact, tend to keep the victim stuck in the anger stage of healing. Restorative justice, with professional mediation between the Church and the victim, could lead to a healing settlement of monetary compensation and payment for the victim's counseling.

Healing apology meetings can also be facilitated between priest abuser, victim, and Church leadership. We see a model for such a program in the Vietnamese Buddhist monk Thich Nhat Hanh's healing retreats for American soldiers, Vietnamese soldiers, and civilians injured or traumatized in the Vietnam War. Another model is the Truth and Reconciliation Commission meetings in South Africa, which brought together victims and perpetrators of the abusive apartheid system for the purpose of speaking out about the abuse, expressing apologies, offering forgiveness, and promoting healing reconciliation.

Some dioceses and religious orders are already using the restorative justice model for victims, offering mediation rather than court battles. Some victim advocate groups, such as the Restorative Justice Council on Sexual Misconduct in Faith Communities and the Healing Alliance, promote this approach as a more healing alternative to the adversarial approach of civil suits and settlements.

SHATTERING MYTHS

Another feature of the new narrative is a new and fuller understanding of victims and survivors as well as priest victim-abusers that refutes the myths and misconceptions often held about both groups. The new story would break the pervasive myth about victims that says they are doomed to be victims their whole lives. As the three stories by victims demonstrate, healing is possible. There is hope. The human spirit is more resilient than we sometimes allow. For many victims, scars will remain. Some others may develop even more strength than they would otherwise have developed. For all, there is an opportunity to transcend what was done to them in the abuse. Victims need not live in despair or shame; healing is available, though the journey may be hard and sometimes long. All that was said above about the opportunity for healing for the victims of abuse can also be said about the victim-abusers. We have seen their capacity for healing in the five stories by priests who are now in recovery. All can move in some way from being a victim to being a survivor or even a thriver.

The new narrative would also shatter the myth that there is no hope for priest abusers. Rather, their illness

213

can be arrested and treated. As with the alcoholic, curing this disease is not possible, but full, ongoing healthy recovery without any sexually compulsive or abusive behavior is achievable. We have seen examples of this in the stories of the five priests in this book. It takes long-term intensive therapy, and it requires a lifetime commitment by the priest to his recovery protocols. It also needs, we believe, some form of lifelong supervision and accountability for maintaining recovery. Most of those we have treated achieve full, healthy recovery. A small minority achieve only partial recovery. A few resist treatment, remain in denial, and continue in their sickness. Yet hope and recovery is possible.

TREATMENT TO END
THE CYCLE OF ABUSE

Treatment of this compulsive sickness involves a number of components. We will highlight only a few here. Treatment needs to include first of all stopping the abusive behavior and removing the priest from active, public ministry. It requires empathic confrontation, consequences, and accountability for the abusive behavior to break through the priest's denial and thought distortions, symptoms that are a part of every addictive disorder. This needs to be done firmly and definitively, yet without toxically shaming the priest. Too often Church leadership or even treatment professionals have shamed these men for their problem. Shaming just sickens them more. Since they are already filled with immense shame, and since toxic shame is one of the triggers for the compulsive behavior, this is counterproductive and even dangerous.

Treatment needs to restore their capacity to feel their emotions and their inner life, which has been numbed by both their own abuse and their addiction. This especially includes the ability to feel finally what they have done to their victims. This is the restoration of empathy, the capacity to emotionally feel the experience of the other and especially to feel the consequences of one's behavior toward the other. This is an incredibly painful and yet necessary process for the priest victim-abuser. He needs to feel fully what he has done to his victim so that he will never repeat such abuse again.

Treatment must also focus on healing the original traumas and abuse experiences that constituted the core and root of a priest abuser's illness. Superficial, fragile, and brittle recovery will result if only the compulsive behaviors are stopped and the core trauma is not treated. This treatment includes the gradual reduction or elimination of toxic shame and the restoration of a healthy and positive sense of self. The priest must finally learn and experience nonabusive and truly intimate healthy relationships and community. Treatment that is condemning or not compassionate reabuses the priest and continues the circle of abuse. His illness will simply go further underground and become more dangerous again.

There can never be any delusion that the recovering priest is cured after a certain length of treatment and he can now resume his old life and ministry. He must establish and live certain recovery practices and protocols for the rest of his life. This must be supervised by appropriate professionals, and a system of accountability and lifetime supervision structures must be put into place. This needs

215

to be designed for the protection of children or other possible victims and also for the health and recovery needs
of the priest.

As we have seen with victims of abuse, treatment cannot just involve psychological healing. It must integrate
spiritual restoration as well. The same three areas of spiritual healing apply to priest victim-abusers as to victims:
forgiveness, discovery of meaning in their suffering and in
the suffering they have caused, and renewed purpose and
some form of service to others. As difficult as it may be
for us, these men need our forgiveness for their healing.
They also need to experience and accept the forgiveness
God offers them. Hardest of all, many times, they need to
eventually forgive themselves. Such a circle of forgiveness
is ultimately liberating for all involved, victim and abuser
alike, breaking the cycle of abuse.

The priest in recovery from this illness must also be
helped to find meaning and new purpose out of the suffering he has caused and experienced. He must discover
spiritual meaning amid the pieces of his now fractured
life and rearrange the pieces into a new life purpose. And
he must find a new way to give service to others. In the
stories of the five priests, we hear some indications of
this process: some of them dedicate their lives to prayer
and penance for their victims; some of them develop a
new compassion for those in need in the world; and some
commit themselves to helping and supporting their fellow
priests in recovery.

A difficult issue that arises here is that, unless he
chooses to leave the priesthood, the recovering priest
will need to find his meaning, new purpose, and service
somehow as a priest. His identity and spirituality are very

216

much tied to his priesthood. Recovery will, then, require some form of healing and renewal of his priesthood. Most of these men will never return to active public ministry. So treatment must involve a reaffirmation and redirection of their priestly call within the limitations necessary in their recovery protocols. Some people object to allowing these priests to continue and function in their priesthood at all, in any way. They believe they have forfeited their right to their priesthood by their abusive actions. However, if they are suffering from an illness and their actions stemmed from this illness and their own victimization, is this just? Is it merciful? For these priests, the loss of their active, public priestly ministry is already a great and painful consequence of their addiction.

The Dallas Charter of 2002 was an attempt by the American Catholic bishops to respond to the growing sexual abuse crisis. Much of it was a helpful and long overdue response to the needs of victims and the protection of children. Part of the charter is the so-called "one strike and you're out" policy, which says that any priest found to have abused a child or adolescent would automatically be forced out of the priesthood.[40] We believe this is neither fair to the priest, nor safe for the community. If, as we have found, the priest who abuses is suffering from an illness originating in his own victimization, is it just to punish him in this way for his illness? If a priest is alcoholic and has a relapse, the Church does not laicize him. If the priest is bipolar and has a serious manic episode, the Church hopefully would not expel him. Certainly the consequences of this illness are far greater for the victims, the Church, and society, so the sanctions and protections need to be greater. However, the Church has a gospel responsibility to its wounded, sickened priests and cannot turn its back on them. If a priest refuses or is unable to establish recovery from his illness, then certainly he must be involuntarily expelled from the priesthood.

In forcibly laicizing these priests, the Church would also be abdicating its responsibility for the safety of children and the community. If these priests are expelled from the priesthood, the Church no longer has any authority to supervise them and their recovery. In many cases, there would be no supervision by civil authorities, and they will live in the community. Without supervision and accountability to the Church, it would be more difficult for them to maintain their recovery, and they would be more susceptible to relapse and to reabuse. Ultimately, recovery is the responsibility of each individual recovering priest; however, their recovery will be stronger, and the community will be safer, if these men are able to remain priests in a system that the Church monitors.

FUTURE PRECAUTIONS

"Is celibacy a part of the problem?" "Would optional celibacy eliminate the problem of abusive priests?" These are frequently asked questions in response to the sexual abuse crisis in the Church. We have our own personal beliefs about the Church changing its tradition and allowing priests to marry. However, that question is beyond the scope and purview of this book. Our clinical experience working with priests who have abused is that celibacy is not the main issue. There is no evidence that celibate clergy are any more likely to become sick in this way and abuse than are married clergy. For some abusive priests celibacy may have been a contributing factor making it more difficult, for instance, to find healthy outlets for the ordinary human need for relational closeness.

However, the real issue is the quality of the screening and preparation of candidates for a celibate priesthood. Most of these men were not prepared properly in their seminary training to live a celibate life. In the old seminary system, few were. For others, it was not a life that fit them well. Celibacy can be a psychosexually healthy and productive way of life. It is not an easy way of life and requires an individual who is psychologically and spiritually mature to live it well (actually, the same could be said of marriage). Seminary formation of future priests has changed considerably. It needs to continue to get better. Candidates for the priesthood need to be taught more than the theological theory of priesthood and celibacy. They also need to be taught practical life skills of how to live celibacy. Screening and formation needs to ensure that future priests are mature and healthy enough to live and thrive as celibates.

In addition, seminarians still are not given sufficient preparation for the healthy and proper use of the role and personal power they will have as priests. Abuse is as much an aberration of power as it is of sex. Nor are candidates educated sufficiently, if at all, about the psychological dynamics of the pastoral relationships they will enter into as priests. There still seems little understanding among candidates and priests of the transference and countertransference issues that frequently enter relationships in the course of ministry. These are situations where the person being ministered to projects a need onto the priest, and the priest in turn projects his need or unresolved psychological issue. Priests, and clergy in general, although excellent at identifying the needs of others and ministering to them, tend to be rather poor at identifying their own personal needs. Consequently, there is a danger that they will act out their needs and inner woundedness, not only in psychosexual issues, with those they minister to. This usually unconscious process is a factor in many of the cases of abuse we have seen.

In the recent movie *The Woodsman,* Kevin Bacon plays a sexual offender released from prison after serving twelve years for molesting a child. He is sincere in his remorse for the abuse and is attempting to put his life back together. He encounters some support, even love, yet also much fear, suspicion, and hate. Rehabilitating his life is an uphill battle. The movie raises the question, how will society respond to sex offenders among us? This book poses that same question in regard to priests who have abused. How can we balance the need to protect our young, which must always be our first priority, with supporting and rehabilitating those priest abusers who are sincerely working to recover from their illness and re-establish a life of meaning, purpose, and service? How we answer this question will determine whether we remain in an old story of denial, secrecy, anger, and shame and judgment that continues the cycle of abuse, or whether we choose to live in a new narrative of truth, openness, protection, empathy, compassion, healing, and hope for all involved, victim and victim-abuser alike.

Constructing a new narrative and putting it into practical terms in Church and societal policies and structures will take time. The stories of these five priests and three survivors, and the many other stories they represent, provide us with some illuminating and hopeful signposts along the way. They teach us about the devastating power of denial, secrecy, shame, the sickness of addiction, and the real nature of the illness behind the headlines of the priest abuse scandal. They display to us the great damage caused by the abuse of power over the vulnerable. They show us how the beauty and divine fire of sexuality, wounded and sickened, can become a destructive force in any of us. They also teach us, though, about the resiliency of the human spirit. They witness to the ever-available potential for healing. They manifest for us our human capacity for redemption and the divine light that is within each of us, even when obscured and buried under great darkness. They teach us the pathway to the resurrection and reemergence of that light, possible for each of us, no matter how powerful or oppressive the darkness may appear.

The following material describes one model that attempts to help develop a new narrative, balancing the protection of children and society and meaningful healing and recovery for priest victim-abusers. It is a residential, supervised, managed recovery community for priests and brothers.

Eleven

A MODEL OF RESIDENTIAL RECOVERY FOR PRIESTS

~~~ ~~~ ~~~

After having read the personal stories of the individual abusers who have told their stories, it would be appropriate to speak about what they are doing with their lives now. Some are members of a residential facility, where I, Mark, am the director, which houses religious priests and brothers who, for a variety of reasons, are no longer able to serve in active ministry. They suffer from emotional issues, psychological disorders, and sexual boundary violations (compulsive, abusive behavior).

In my clinical experience I have observed that the average age of a priest or brother accused of a sexual boundary violation is in the upper fifties or early sixties. These individuals entered into the seminary in their early teens. Every aspect of their life became dependent upon the institution of the Church. They were taught to interact and perform within a system based upon obedience and submission to the will of the Church authorities. This hierarchical system can create a very dependent mindset. If it is deemed necessary for an individual to seek treatment for either emotional or sexual boundary violations, his immediate superiors order him to go.

ARRIVING AT THE FACILITY

Most of the men who reside at our facility have already completed an extensive three- to six-month inpatient program. These individuals are thoroughly tested and analyzed to determine the extent of their emotional, psychological, or sexual disorder, and their level of commitment to the recovery process, their overall understanding of the consequences of their actions, and their ability to "own" their own behavior. They have completed intensive treatment, and the aftercare recommendation was that they live in a setting that will monitor their recovery. The majority of these individuals have not been accused of a criminal offense. Most are either in the process of some civil allegation or have no legal issues at the present time. Therefore, most of these individuals are theoretically free to live anywhere because they have not been convicted of any crime. In sending these priests and brothers to our facility, I believe the Church has taken a positive and proactive stance in the placement of these men in a setting that provides for their ongoing recovery and the safety of the community.

Most of these individuals come to our program with great resistance. Some are still in denial about their actions. However, each individual must eventually face the reality of the consequences of his actions and accept the fact that he will never be able to be placed in a position of religious authority again.

The first few months after an individual arrives at our facility are usually met with depression and a tremendous feeling of loss, loss of personal freedoms, loss of family, and loss of participating in active ministry. His whole life has been dramatically changed and uprooted. He is in a state of shock. His denial system has maintained, up until now, that he has done nothing wrong. His whole world has come to a crashing halt, and the realization begins to set in that his life as he knew it is completely gone. Along with this strong feeling of loss comes a feeling of abandonment. These individuals who come to our facility have little or no chance of returning to life within their diocese or religious community. This is a hard concept for them to fully understand and accept. Since the majority of these individuals entered the seminary when they were in their early teens, they look upon their diocese and religious community as their family. To be placed in a monitored facility away from their religious family naturally creates feelings of abandonment.

A SENSE OF RESPONSIBILITY

Each individual arrives with a treatment plan and recommendations from his previous inpatient treatment program. It is very important that these recommendations be followed and adhered to upon his arrival. The individual's level of depression is of special concern. Due to the inpatient's feelings of loss and isolation, suicidal ideation needs to be strongly observed. A psychiatrist monitors his medications, and he meets regularly with a therapist trained in the area of addictions and sexually abusive behavior. Each individual must also sign a release form that allows the program director, therapists, and his religious superiors to discuss his recovery. This open system reduces the amount of manipulation and mind games that are inherent with the addictive personality. This communication also serves as a safeguard against the possibility of a potential relapse.

The first goal is to get the individual, now resident, situated with his therapy and responsibilities. Each resident is also required to attend individual and group therapy. The group helps to generate peer support and encouragement for the recovery process. The peers also help a new resident come to grips with his new living situation, lessen isolation, and decrease the feelings of depression. Pat and Sue run this group on a weekly basis. Their experience, with both victims and perpetrators, helps to bring a good balance for the men to learn and grow through their recovery.

Along with therapy, residents are required to take responsibility for their current living situation. All residents must help with the daily upkeep of the facility. Tasks are assigned to each based upon a person's talents. For example, if a resident enjoys yard work he may be asked to mow the lawn. I stress to the residents that this is their home, and there are no maids or cleaning service.

Having residents maintain the facility is important for two reasons. First, an individual is forced to focus on something other than himself and his depression. These individuals can easily see themselves as victims, which prevents many from moving forward in a positive direction. Giving an individual a sense of ownership of his living situation provides him with purpose and motivation. However, dealing with sometimes emotionally fragile individuals can be a real test of one's patience and fortitude. Some residents take on a rebellious attitude toward their religious authorities and me, especially if they feel forced into this living situation.

Second, responsibility reduces the dependency issues that many of these individuals have acquired over the years. Feelings of dependency only increase the feelings of shame and helplessness that have fueled their addictive and abusive behaviors. Recovery equals responsibility. Without responsibility in their lives, these individuals will continue in a downward spiral. Many of these men have been living under conditions where others provided for their essential needs.

How to gain independence in a closed, dependent environment? The majority of these residents have lost all outside interests due to their emotional problems or sexually abusive behavior. Their past behavior became all-consuming, both emotionally and physically. Developing healthy interests is key to their recovery process and the overall well-being of the resident. We all need to have goals or we become stagnant in life. Giving the residents small and incremental self-fulfilling goals keeps them moving forward in a positive direction. It is important to note that these goals and interests must be confined to the property on which they live. It is a small world, but many of the residents find purpose and contentment here.

Acceptance of living in a monitored residential facility comes with time and work. A resident who is fully integrated and accepting of his situation has structure and purpose to his day. Living isolated and removed from contact with society and their religious brothers can make the days very long. With no public ministry at their disposal, the residents only have the opportunity to minister to each other. To witness the residents reaching out to one another and using their special gifts and talents is very rewarding. To see an individual resident reach out to another resident is to witness a transformation and healing of the self-focus his addiction had created.

Some residents have adapted well to living within our facility. They fully accept the circumstances that placed them in this facility, and they want to bring peace and reconciliation into their lives. Whether they have turned a talent for woodworking into creating beautiful furniture for others as a labor of healing, overcome an inability to form emotional attachments and started caring for the elderly and ailing resident population, or found beauty and purpose in the simple act of caring for the lawn, many of these men have truly grown beyond the confines of their past. They truly want the victims of their abuse to find healing, and they pray for forgiveness from both the victims and God.

One man illustrates this very well. He has been at our facility for approximately ten years. He is a diocesan priest who needed a place of residence that would monitor him because of his past sexual boundary violations. He was in his early seventies upon his arrival, and the actions of his past behavior affected him both emotionally and physically. He experienced both depression and anger, which limited his interaction with the other residents. With therapy and spiritual guidance he slowly worked through his pain and the pain he caused his victims. He was a talented craftsman who worked in a shop on the property and made various pieces of furniture. He began making items only for his own living space, but other residents asked him to build things for their rooms and other areas of the main house. His woodworking became something that connected him with the other residents. This work lifted his guilt and shame concerning his past behavior. He had remorse and felt empathy for his victims, but did not know how to reach out to them and their pain. He took it upon himself to build an altar for the chapel located on the property. It was a labor of healing. He purchased the oak wood himself, working laboriously on the project for over a year. The altar is still in the chapel today, and on it private Mass, with only residents in attendance, is celebrated daily for the healing of victims. His talents were instrumental in his own recovery and the recovery of others in the residence.

I have chosen to involve myself in this work because I feel that I truly have a vocation for dealing with the population that is housed at our facility. I am not aware of many others who want to pursue such an undertaking. I must personally thank my ministry partner and true friend, Rev. Bertin Miller, OFM, who had the foresight and fortitude to envision our program long before the scandals broke out in the Catholic Church. We met before the program officially started, and I was instantly and continue to be impressed by his loving faith. He has worked with priests who have needed his help, both spiritually and mentally, for the majority of his priestly vocation. We have had to weather many storms in our program's history, and I look to him for encouragement and strength as we pursue our mission of healing. He is a true blessing to my family.

The ultimate goal of our program is healing, for the abuser and for the victim. It is easy to sit back and criticize, but how difficult it is to try and do something positive about this heated and painful subject. This facility is one step toward bridging the divide between perpetrators and victims, where a healing model can be developed that is open and acceptable to all parties.

NOTES

1. Ronald Rolheiser, OMI, *The Holy Longing: Guidelines for a Christian Spirituality* (New York: Doubleday, 1999), 193.

2. Richard D. Laws, ed., *Relapse Prevention with Sex Offenders* (New York: Guilford Press, 1989), 80; Patrick Carnes, *Don't Call It Love: Recovery from Sexual Addiction* (New York: Bantam Books, 1990), 109; A. W. Richard Sipe, *Sex, Priests, and Power: Anatomy of a Crisis* (New York: Brunner/Mazel, 1995), 17; Thomas G. Plante, "Priests Behaving Badly: What Do We Know about Priest Sex Offenders?" *Sex Addiction and Compulsivity: The Journal of Treatment and Prevention* 10, nos. 2–3 (2003): 95.

3. Plante, "Priests Behaving Badly," 94–95; Gerald J. McGlone, "Prevalence and Incidence of Roman Catholic Clerical Sex Offenders," *Sex Addiction and Compulsivity: The Journal of Treatment and Prevention* 10, nos. 2–3 (2003): 116–18.

4. John Bradshaw, *Homecoming: Reclaiming and Championing Your Inner Child* (New York: Bantam Books, 1990), 47.

5. Patrick Carnes, *The Betrayal Bond* (Deerfield Beach, FL: Health Communications, 1997), 1–26.

6. William Wordsworth, from the poem "My Heart Leaps Up," *The Norton Anthology of Poetry* (New York: W. W. Norton, 1975), 601.

7. Bradshaw, *Homecoming,* 10.

8. Laws, *Relapse Prevention with Sex Offenders,* 80; Carnes, *Don't Call It Love,* 109; Sipe, *Sex, Priests, and Power,* 17; Plante, "Priests Behaving Badly," 95.

9. Sipe, *Sex, Priests, and Power,* 25.

10. Ibid.

11. Carnes, *The Betrayal Bond,* 24–26.

12. Plante, "Priests Behaving Badly," 95.

13. McGlone, "Prevalence and Incidence of Roman Catholic Clerical Sex Offenders," 112–13.

14. Ibid.; Plante, "Priests Behaving Badly," 93–97.

15. McGlone, "Prevalence and Incidence of Roman Catholic Clerical Sex Offenders," 112–13.

16. Ibid., 111–21.

17. Ibid.

18. Ibid.

19. Ibid.; Sipe, *Sex, Priests, and Power,* 27.

20. Plante, "Priests Behaving Badly," 93–97.

21. Originally written in Middle English by an unknown mystic of the fourteenth century, *The Cloud of Unknowing* and *The Book of Privy Counseling* are available in multiple editions and translations. They represent the first expression in our own tongue of the soul's quest for God and are considered classics of mystical theology. One such edition that is available is edited by William Johnston and includes a foreword by Huston Smith. Anonymous, William Johnston, ed., *The Cloud of Unknowing and The Book of Privy Counseling* (New York: Doubleday/Image, 1973).

22. Ibid.

23. EMDR is an acronym for Eye Movement Desensitization and Reprocessing. It is a therapeutic method "strongly recommended" by the American Psychiatric Association (2004) for the treatment of patients with acute stress disorder and post-traumatic stress disorder. See *www.emdr.com.*

24. Carnes, *Don't Call It Love,* 68.

25. Ibid., 9–38.

26. Plante, "Priests Behaving Badly," 95.

27. Marie Fortune, *Is Nothing Sacred?* (San Francisco: Harper-Collins, 1989), 38.

28. Malcolm Muggeridge, *Something Beautiful for God* (New York: HarperCollins, 1971).

29. Fortune, *Is Nothing Sacred?* 122.

30. Macrina Wiederkehr, OSB, *Behold Your Life* (Notre Dame, IN: Ave Maria Press, 2000), 15. "I called through your door" is reprinted from *The Essential Rumi,* trans. Coleman Barks. Copyright 1997, Threshold Books.

31. Joan Chittister, *Scarred by Struggle, Transformed by Hope* (Grand Rapids, MI: Wm. B. Eerdmans, 2003), 89–90.

32. Richard Rohr, OFM, *Everything Belongs* (New York: Crossroad, 1999, 2003).

33. Viktor Frankl, *Man's Search for Meaning* (New York: Pocket Books, 1959).

34. Carnes, *The Betrayal Bond,* 143.

35. More information about the principles of AA can be found in *Alcoholics Anonymous* (New York: Alcoholics Anonymous World Services, Inc., 1976).

36. See Fred Luskin, *Forgive for Good* (New York, Harper-Collins, 2002), a book which compiles the psychological and medical and scientific research from the Stanford Forgiveness Project; see also Lewis B. Smedes, *Forgive and Forget* (San Francisco: HarperCollins, 1984); Gerald G. Jampolsky, *Forgiveness* (Hillsboro, OR: Beyond Words Publishing, 1999); Desmond Tutu, *No Future without Forgiveness* (New York: Doubleday, 1999).

37. See *www.athealth.com* about the nature of resilience. Some longitudinal studies, several of which follow individuals over the course of a lifespan, have consistently documented that between half and two-thirds of children growing up in families with mentally ill, alcoholic, abusive, or criminally involved parents or in poverty-stricken or war-torn communities do overcome the odds and turn a life trajectory of risk into one that manifests "resilience," the term used to describe a set of qualities that foster a process of successful adaptation and transformation despite risk and adversity. Resilience research validates prior research and theory in human development that has clearly established the biological imperative for growth and development that exists in the human organism and that unfolds naturally in the presence of certain environmental characteristics. We are all born with an innate capacity for resilience,

by which we are able to develop social competence, problem-solving skills, a critical consciousness, autonomy, and a sense of purpose.

38. Virginia Satir, *The New Peoplemaking* (Mountain View, CA: Science and Behavior Books, 1988), 340.

39. Theorists and psychotherapists in the field of narrative therapy include Michael White, Lynn Hoffman, David Epston, Jill Friedman, Kathie Crockett, Gene Combs, Wendy Drewery, John Winslade, and Glen J. Simblett. See, for example, *Narrative Therapy in Practice: The Archeology of Hope,* ed. Crockett, Winslade, Epston, and Monk (San Francisco: Jossey-Bass, 1997).

40. When the sexual abuse crisis exploded in the Archdiocese of Boston, there was a ripple effect on the entire Catholic Church in the United States. The response of the U.S. Conference of Catholic Bishops was the approval of the Charter for the Protection of Children and Young People at the spring meeting of 2002 in Dallas. See *www.usccb.org,* which is the website for the U.S. Conference of Catholic Bishops, for more information.

RECOMMENDED RESOURCES

If you have been abused by a Catholic religious leader, or if you know someone who has been abused, please contact one of the following resources:

Link-Up — The Healing Alliance
P.O. Box 429
Pewee Valley, KY 40056
502-241-5544
Web site: *www.thelinkup.org*
Susan Archibald, President

Restorative Justice Council on Sexual Misconduct
in Faith Communities
2233 University Avenue West
St. Paul, MN 55114
612-874-0535
Web site: *www.rjcouncil.org*
Linda Harvey, Program Director

Pathways to Hope
205 W. Monroe St.
Chicago, IL 60606
312-223-1085
866-784-5900
Web site: *www.pathwaystohope.com*
Jennifer Reed, Executive Director

Most Catholic dioceses and religious orders now have a committee composed of lay and clergy professionals focused on ministering to the needs of clergy sexual abuse victims. Contact your local diocese or the office of the provincial if a religious order is involved.

ACKNOWLEDGMENTS

My heart is grateful for many things. First of all, I am grateful for my children, Joe, Mary, Gerry, Cindy, and Louise (and their wonderful spouses, Cherlyn, Angie, Arnie, and Jack), who were and continue to be my teachers in unconditional love and how to laugh at myself. I especially want to thank Louise and Cindy for their honest and insightful feedback about the manuscript. I am grateful also for our grandchildren, Jason, Chris, John, Sammi, Kevin, Maggie, Erin, Michelle, and Nicole. Each of you personifies Sacred Joy.

I am thankful to all my clients these past twenty-two years who have trusted me with their stories and pain and have shown such courage as they entered their healing path, one step at a time. Thank you, each one of you. I want also to acknowledge my late teacher, mentor, and friend, Virginia Satir. Thank you for seeing the bright light within me, which was so surrounded by darkness, for mirroring that light to me, and helping me to bring it forth.

Finally, I am deeply grateful to my best friend, partner, and husband, Patrick. You love me for who God has created me to be, and I am grateful. Thank you.

(Sue Lauber-Fleming)

I am grateful beyond words to my best friend, wife, partner, cotherapist, and now coauthor, Sue, for the many years of fun, adventure, spiritual journeying, support, challenge, work, and love we have shared. I am especially indebted to Sue for her challenge to write, repeated over many years, a challenge to which I am finally responding. Without her encouragement and support, this book would never have happened. I want also to express my appreciation to Mark, my coauthor and director of the program at Recon. His trust in me, my work as a counselor, and our collaboration in this project have been highlights of my professional life.

I want to acknowledge Sr. Mary Peace Howard, PhD, for her many years of friendship and personal and professional support for this work. Thanks as well to her whole community, the Companions in the Infinite Love, whose prayer, support, and contemplative hospitality made the work of writing this book a great deal easier. I want to thank my therapy clients over the last twenty-two years, who have entrusted their hearts and souls to me, and who have taught me so much about hope, courage, and our human capacity to heal and change.   (Patrick Fleming)

I would like to first thank my wife, Candy, who worked long and hard at typing and compiling the original manuscript that was sent to our publisher. This was tedious work that helped pull all our material together. She is a wonderful mother to our children, Morgan and Ryan, and she is very supportive of me and my work. It is through both Candy and my children that I experience unconditional love on a daily basis. They bring both balance and support into my life, which helps me deal with my always challenging, and sometimes stressful, ministry.

I also want to thank my dear friend and partner in ministry, Fr. Bert Miller, OFM. He has been and continues to be a mentor to me and has allowed me to be part of his vision of establishing a residential program for priests and religious who can no longer function within active ministry. He has truly given me the freedom to do what I do best. Finally, I need to thank both of my parents for providing me with a family which was filled with love and commitment. Their strength and love for one another continue to guide me throughout the days of my life.   (Mark T. Matousek)

Together, we want to acknowledge and thank our anonymous coauthors whose stories are the heart of this book. We thank you for the courage and openness you have shown in telling your story and giving us all a window into your personal journeys from pain and despair into healing and hope. We want to thank Paula D'Arcy for her crucial early support and encouragement. We want to express our deep appreciation to Dr. Gwendolin Herder, Publisher and CEO of The Crossroad Publishing Company, and to Dr. John Jones, Editorial Director, for believing in this book. You saw its "authentic hope" in the midst of a dark and controversial chapter in the history of the Church and have the courage to publish what you saw.

Finally, we want to thank Roy M. Carlisle, our Senior Editor at Crossroad, for patiently shepherding three first-time authors through the ins and outs and ups and downs of the publishing maze. Thank you for your patience, teaching, wisdom, expertise, and spirit, and for your faith in us and in what we are intending to accomplish in this book.

We feel blessed that our paths have crossed with all of these people and many others that God has brought into our lives.

ABOUT THE AUTHORS

Sue Lauber-Fleming, RN, MA, LCSW, is a psychotherapist in private practice with her husband, Patrick Fleming,
in St. Louis. She trained extensively with family therapy
pioneer Virginia Satir. She has over twenty years of experience working with individuals and groups and addressing
a variety of psychological problems. The focus of her work
has been bringing healing to adult survivors of childhood
sexual abuse, including those abused by clergy. She is
herself a survivor of clerical sexual abuse. In more recent years, she has been providing group and individual
counseling to priests who have abused. Sue has been
a psychological and organizational consultant to several
Catholic religious communities, including teaching and
facilitating year-long community-building classes for the
international novitiate of a religious order of men for the
past twelve years. She is the proud mother of five and
grateful "granny" of nine wonderful grandchildren.

Patrick Fleming, MDiv, MSW, LCSW, CSAT, is a psychotherapist in private practice with his wife, Sue Lauber-Fleming,
in St. Louis. He trained extensively with Patrick Carnes,
PhD, an international expert and researcher in the field of
sexual addiction. Patrick Fleming has over twenty years of
experience in providing counseling to individuals, couples,
and groups facing a wide variety of psychological problems, including male and female adult victims of childhood

sexual abuse, some of these victims of clerical abuse. In the last fifteen years, he has specialized in working with those suffering from sexual compulsivity and addiction. He is a Certified Sexual Addiction Therapist. This work led him to work extensively with priests and other clergy, Catholic and Protestant, who have abused. Patrick is also a former parish priest and hospital chaplain. With Sue, he enjoys the life and energy of their nine grandchildren.

Sue Lauber-Fleming and Patrick Fleming are cofounders of Double Rainbow Coaching, Counseling and Consulting, their private practice dedicated to interweaving psychology with faith and spirituality in promoting the healing and growth of individuals and groups. They together provide group and individual psychotherapy to recovering Catholic priests and brothers at the Recon program outside of St. Louis.

Mark T. Matousek, MS, CCDC, was born and raised in Bayside, New York. He graduated from Cathedral Preparatory Seminary High School and earned a Masters Degree in Rehabilitation Counseling from St. John's University. He has focused his work in the area of addictions and earned his CCDC (Certified Chemical Dependency Counselor) certification. He was the administrator of an inpatient drug and alcohol program in Maryland and also worked for the American Cancer Society. Mark relocated to Missouri to become the director of clinical services of Recon, Inc. He has been with the Recon program for thirteen years. He works closely with the staff of Recon in assisting and educating the Catholic Church regarding the problems of sexual abuse and the need for permanent residency programs for post-offenders.

Of Related Interest

John J. Dietzen
CATHOLIC Q & A
Answers to the Most Common Questions
about Catholicism

Three features make this book unique.

It is comprehensive and current. These hundreds of questions are drawn from real-life questions Fr. Dietzen has received over the years from readers and parishioners, and new questions are added for every edition to reflect current trends and issues.

It is Catholic. Fr. Dietzen shows what the official church teaching is, as well as where church teaching is silent. This Crossroad edition will also carry the imprimatur, as earlier editions did.

It is compassionate. Fr. Dietzen writes with an engaging and warm pastoral style to convey the joy and wisdom of the Catholic faith.

Fr. Dietzen has been a columnist for the Catholic News Service since 1975.

ISBN 0-8245-2309-1, paper

Check your local bookstore for availability.
To order directly from the publisher,
please call 1-800-707-0670 for Customer Service
or visit our Web site at *www.cpcbooks.com.*
For catalog orders, please send your request
to the address below.

THE CROSSROAD PUBLISHING COMPANY
16 Penn Plaza, Suite 1550
New York, NY 10001

crossroad